The Songwriter's Guide to the Galaxy

The Songwriter's Guide to the Galaxy

Tiff Lacey

© PeaChi Publishing
www.peachip.co.uk
Morants Court • Chevening
Kent, United Kingdom

First published 2014

ISBN: 978-0-9928968-0-5

Table of Contents

Preface

"If music be the food of love, play on; give me excess of it, that, surfeiting, the appetite may sicken, and so die." (William Shakespeare – Twelfth Night)

I t feels like I have written songs all my life.

At least, I have done so, from a very early age. Heaped with bravado but lacking in confidence, I hid my light under a bushel for many years until I finally found the courage to dip my toe into industry water.

Since then I have accumulated over 25 years of industry knowledge and experience.

If like me, you are easily distracted or not keen on reading because you would prefer to **get on creating**, then **happy days**, this book is for you. You will find no verbal padding as I have tried to keep the text succinct and to the point. You can of course skip to the penultimate chapter, **Protection and Pitfalls**, but you might miss something crucial that could benefit or apply just to you, so I hope you make it all the way through.

On a legal note, contained within these pages is my opinion, findings, knowledge and the lessons learned from a career spanning over three decades.

This book is an overview of the Music Industry. However, no warranty whatsoever is made that the information contained herein is accurate and some facts may have changed since going to publication. There is absolutely no assurance that any statement contained in this book, especially those touching on legal matters, is true and correct. Law is amended, modified or overturned over time and it may only be accurate in a certain territory.

The information provided herein cannot substitute professional advice. Therefore no responsibility will be taken for the results or consequences of any attempt to use or adopt any of the information or disinformation presented in this publication.

I do hope you enjoy reading this book and that it inspires you toward your path to success.

So you want to be a Singer/Songwriter?

"I was born with music inside me. Music was one of my parts. Like my ribs, my kidneys, my liver, my heart. Like my blood. It was a force already within me when I arrived on the scene. It was a necessity for me, like food or water." (Ray Charles) :

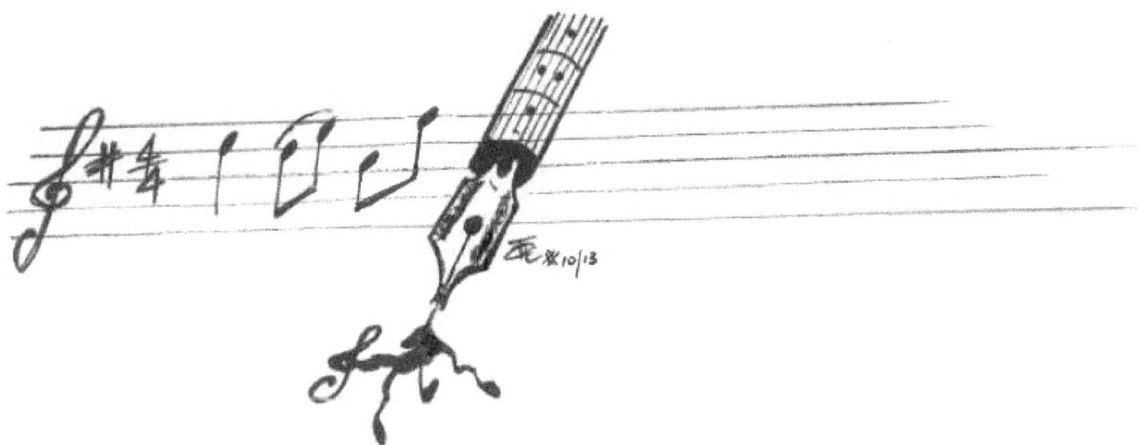

It can be a daunting view, looking in from the outside at the Music Industry. With so many levels and elements to distinguish from, I decided that this book would focus primarily on the view of the Singer/Songwriter.

Contained within these pages, you will find information that could be extremely beneficial to you before you embark on your musical adventures.

What kind of Artist do you want to be?

Do you envisage yourself rocking up on stage and kicking off your career as the next Madonna, Rihanna, Beyoncé, Robbie Williams, Adele, Michael Bublé, Nicole Scherzinger, Tinie Tempah or Katy Perry? Or does the solo life fill you with dread? Would you prefer the solidarity of being in a band, like that of Chris Martin, Emma Bunton, Bono, Tom Meighan, Justine Frischmann or Harry Styles?

You may want to write songs for other people and avoid the hustle and bustle of the limelight? Creating toplines (musical hooks) for other Artists/Bands?

Perhaps none of these career paths appeal to you? Would you feel more comfortable behind the scenes, working on albums or projects with other Artists/Bands, as a Session Singer/Musician?

Being in a Band

I always enjoyed the camaraderie of being in a band.

I felt there was something spiritual in jamming or writing a new song and then learning it with the Band. Technically, as a Band, you are all **in it** together, like work colleagues or partners in a company. However, from a legal standpoint this is **not** the case and many a Band has split up due to this small detail not being taken care of from the very start. Unless you have proof of your songwriting, or more appropriately, a written songwriting/collaboration agreement setting out your share of the songwriting (especially if you are **not** involved in writing the songs), your fellow members do not have **ANY** obligation to pay you for your contribution.

As a Band, you will **all** need to be focused and all Band Members driving in the same direction both musically and professionally. Even the most ambitious and dedicated Band may still hit the odd hurdle. There are many common stumbling blocks, a Band Member who is lethargic and drags the rest of the Band down or Band Members wanting to go in a different musical direction. Either way, obstacles such as these will slow your progress and leave you feeling like you are treading water.

A Band should develop style from both a musical and a fashion standpoint so that you can market yourselves. Unless you have Management, your marketing tactic should include promotional material (**EPK** (Electronic Press Kit)) which should incorporate a show reel (a CD or electronic MP3) that features three to four of your best songs,

Band photographs, Band biography (your Musical CV), any gig reviews you may have and links to the Band's website and social media websites.

It is worth noting that before sending out any original material you should take the necessary provisions to copyright your work, as set out in **Chapter 13, Copyright Protection**.

Management

If a Band decides to sign a Contract with Management there are certain aspects that should be considered. Firstly, a Management Contract should contain mutual assurances and guarantees. Depending on the resources Management are offering will have an impact as to what roles the Band can expect to be undertaken by any prospective Management. Theoretically this could have an influence on the percentage that Management would expect to receive. For a Band just starting out, 20%-25% (twenty to twenty-five per cent.) is usual. However, this can be negotiated at a reducing rate pending achievements attained by Management. As with all contracts, you are recommended to seek advice from a Solicitor who can clarify issues within the Contract and possibly help you negotiate the deal.

Management can be an individual, a small independent practice or a large multifaceted company. Management should act as a representative, directing the Band's career. They should be involved and committed to oversee day-to-day affairs, business and professional matters for the Band including short and long-term strategies, professional developments and decisions.

When Management is an individual, it is worth remembering that they may have to **wear many hats** and act in multiple roles: from Publicist, Promoter, Accountant to Personal Assistant. This type of arrangement can be effective where a Band is an unknown entity, as the work involved in promoting, booking and touring are typically minimal while Management builds the Band's profile. That is, provided Management represent only one or two acts.

In the case of an established Band, touring, promotion and day-to-day schedules can be hectic. It may be that the Band will require the support of Management who have a wealth of resources thus enabling Management to advance the Band further along their career path.

It may seem a great idea to leave the seemingly mundane tasks to your Management. **BUT**, it is worth noting that if you have no experience of the Music Industry you will not gain any knowledge of it without a modicum of involvement.

A great example of this is the Boy Band, **Bros**. On December 1986, twin brothers **Luke** and **Matt Goss** (**Bros**) walked into **Tom Watkin's** office.

Knowing of **Watkin's** success with **Pet Shop Boys**, they viewed him, as did many in the industry, as a marketing guru. Sure enough, with **Watkin's** help, **Bros** assured themselves ultimate pop stardom.

Off the back of his reputation **Watkins** negotiated and signed a Contract with **Bros** that guaranteed him 20% (twenty per cent.) of **any** of **Bros'** gross earnings. Within a short amount of time **Bros** were a household name and the money poured into **Watkin's** bank account.

Bros were a chart success, their album **Push** reached No. 2 in the UK making several million pounds. However, what the Band failed to realise was that they had been living entirely on credit throughout their 18 months of stardom.

They had been ill advised.

Their tours cost a fortune and barely broke even.

Unaware of any of the financial aspects of their career, **Bros'** spending took them into the red.

They were barely in their twenties when they found themselves penniless, up to their ears in debt and part of pop history.

Meanwhile **Watkins'** career and earnings flourished as he went on to manage **East 17**.[1]

BUT it is not just the young and naïve who make bad decisions.

Aerosmith who had already been ripped off by their earlier Management failed to read the small print before they signed a new Management Contract with **Leber** and **Krebs**. **Leber** and

---

[1] *This information was taken from an article in The Independent by Jim White in 1993.*

Krebs had put a provision into the Contract which signed over **ALL** publishing from **Aerosmith** to them. Needless to say **Leber** and **Krebs** amassed a fortune on this slight technicality[2].

Publishing

In an ideal world, as a Band, **all** Band Members should equally share the publishing royalties. **Unless** you have signed an Agreement setting this out, there is no surety that you will be paid any publishing royalties if you are not the main Songwriter or a Co-writer.

In the instance of **Spandau Ballet**: **Gary Kemp** was the main Songwriter for the band.

No formal agreement had been drawn up but **Kemp**, who took the credit but initially not all the proceeds, paid the other members a share of his income for a certain time. However, when this arrangement came to an end, three members of the band, **Tony Hadley**, **Steve Norman** and **John Keeble** launched a legal battle against **Kemp**. They told the Court that they felt they were still entitled to a share of **Kemp's** publishing royalties which included the hits **True** and **Gold**. **Hadley**, **Norman** and **Keeble** were unsuccessful in their legal action. It was a bitter pill to swallow because they all genuinely believed a verbal agreement had been put in place in 1980 entitling each of them to receive one-twelfth of all the song royalties. They were convinced their involvement in the recordings of the songs would automatically entitle them to a share of the publishing rights.

Unfortunately, the judge ruled *"that although they had made impressive and excellent contributions, they did not alter the songs enough to make them joint authors"*.

On hearing the news, **Hadley** said he was very disappointed: *"Let this be a serious lesson to any up and coming artist or band. No matter how good mates you are or whether you were at school together, get a contract."*[3]

---

[2] *This information was taken from a blog by LA Weekly.*

[3] *This information was taken from an Article in The Independent by Kate Watson-Smyth in 1999.*

Singer / Songwriter

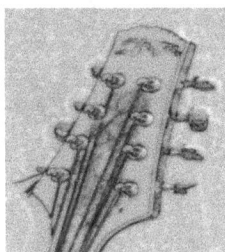

As a Singer/Songwriter you have artistic freedom. You can create songs that make personal statements about yourself, the world and its Aunt or you can bang out cheese-royale pop song after pop song.

This may seem an easy decision but you may be surprised that as soon as you set your stall out as a Singer/Songwriter, you get offers to sing other Songwriter's songs and over time you may become inundated by offers of:

"I have just written the most perfect song for your voice"

"Your style is not really commercial, you need to sing my song then you will get the break you truly deserve"

"I love your voice, it would be a dream come true if you would sing on my track"

"You're a great Singer, it's what you do best but just leave the songwriting to me, it's what I do best"

These old chestnuts and many more like them, may tickle, tempt or just plain annoy you.

And it really is never as simple as making one decision in life and sticking to it. As time goes by, the winds of change lure us in other directions and certain situations may make us feel differently later down the road. The Music Industry is a small pond and if you stick to your guns, word will soon get out what **you are** and what you **are not** prepared to suffer for your art.

But there is good news, the **choice** is **yours** and the first choice you may have to make is whether you go it alone or form a Band.

So, if you do not have a **ready-made five piece** at your disposal, you may have to audition Band Members or audition to become a **Band Member** yourself. As a Singer/Songwriter in a Band, your fellow Band Members will need to be kindred spirits. You will all need to have the same target: drive, ambition and self-belief, because if you do not like **your songs** then how do you expect the buying public to **LOVE** them. This is imperative if your goal is public attention.

One issue I feel that should be brought to your attention (a subject prevalent to the **EDM** genre and one which has come under scrutiny of late) is the use of the title **featuring** (i.e. DJ Fuzzy Fuzz featuring Asinger). It may be that if you write or sing on a track that the Record Label lists the track with you **featuring**. The reason for the use of this title is because most Record Labels will have signed a DJ, Producer or Artist/Band directly to their Record Label and will only focus on promoting their client (the DJ, Producer or Artist/Band).

So why does the term **featuring** exist? Originally the term was used because it was usual for an Artist to **feature** on a record if they were collaborating either outside of their Band or as a solo Artist working with another Artist. This worked quite effectively when both Artists were signed to individual Record Labels.

In today's market, using the term **featuring** can be misleading and may also leave a negative connotation. Insofar that the Record Label's **DJ, Producer** or **Artist/Band** is promoted but the **featured** Singer/Artist is portrayed almost in a secondary rank.

How ironic, when on a lot of occasions, the **featured** Singer/Artist has co-written the track. So this branding seems quite unfair.

Over the past year or so, many established Singer/Songwriters within the EDM genre have insisted that track titles now list them equally, i.e. Artist **and** Artist or Artist **versus** Artist, thereby no distinction or disparity occurs between collaborators.

However, if you are a Singer/Songwriter and you are in a Band, then you may feel this title is more appropriate being used in its original context and thereby distinguishing you from any work outside your Band.

Either way, the jury is still out and basically, use of the term **featuring** is down to preference and will depend on how you view the title. If you have Management, this is something that Management should deal with for you on your behalf.

As a Singer/Songwriter, if you intend to get your own Record Deal you will need promotional material (**EPK**[4]). Your EPK should include three or four of your best tracks, professional photographs, biography (your Musical CV), any gig or track reviews and links to all your web pages.

Once you have your EPK, you can send it to the A&R Representatives of Record Labels you feel would take an interest and could possibly sign you. It is worth noting, that some Record Labels may want an established fan base. Creating a website and promoting yourself or your Band via social media feeds will help you build both your profile and your fan base.

---

[4] Electronic Press Kit

Please note, that before handing or sending out any of your original material, you should make sure your work is properly protected. You will find out how to do this in **Chapter 13, Copyright Protection**.

Ed Sheeran amassed much of his 3 million fan base through Facebook and Twitter. Relentless gigging and working extremely hard for many years, he recorded numerous EPs and got to No #2 in the iTunes charts. **Sheeran** also received millions of hits for his track **You Need Me** resulting in support from **Radio 1** and **1Extra** so that when Asylum/Atlantic Records (who are part of Warner Music Group) offered him a deal, he was able to negotiate more advantageous terms than a typical contract.[5]

Management

If you (your Band) have signed a Management Contract then Management should market and promote your work.

Management should help to direct your career, set up gigs, make sure you get paid, deal with Record Labels and ultimately ensure you get that all-encompassing Record Deal. Management will either **work** or **not work** for you. In my experience, I found Management can get in the way of the creative process. In some cases, Management may try to tell you what you should be writing or singing and from an artistic standpoint that can be extremely off-putting. Also, if said newly appointed Management is not singing from the same hymn sheet as you (meaning, their idea of global domination is you opening up the local chip shop on a rainy Wednesday night or playing at your Local Conservative Club for the next fifty years), then having Management is not going to bode well for you. But, if you contract with someone who is driven, has your back, knows the industry from top to bottom complete with a black book filled with important contacts then you are onto a winner.

In **Bob Dylan's** case, **Albert Grossman** (who was an iconic folk manager at the time) signed a Management Contract with **Dylan** for ten years.

---

[5] *This information was taken from an article on The Guardian Music Blog by Helienne Lindvall on 2 February 2012.*

However, **Grossman** abused his position by taking 25% (twenty-five per cent.) of **Dylan's** earnings when at the time, 15% (fifteen per cent.) was the Music Industry norm.

To add insult to injury, **Grossman** also kept a huge percentage of **Dylan's** publishing rights. This was at a time when many other artists had complete control of their own publishing. As you can imagine, **Dylan** was **Grossman's** biggest client. Realising he was getting ripped off, an irate **Dylan** cut all ties with **Grossman**, although the case was not legally settled until many years later.[6]

Publishing

From a publishing aspect, as a Singer/Songwriter, you are entitled to all (or a percentage of) the publishing (depending on whether you have written the song entirely alone or have collaborated with another writer). Meaning that if you wrote the song in its entirety, on your own, the publishing is 100% (one hundred per cent.) owned by you.

However, if you co-wrote the song with another Songwriter then the percentage you own of the publishing will depend upon what you initially agreed (typically 50/50 if between two parties). It is a common myth that the royalty is split equally between Band Members. This is not correct unless a Band has agreed that this will be the case.

Rumour has it that both **U2** and **Coldplay** share their royalties equally between all Band Members.

However, on the other side of the royalty coin, I read a quote that said the publishing royalty for **Roxy Music** changed from song to song.

So unless you are writing solo, it is good to get into the habit of signing a Songwriting Agreement, before things get too hectic and everyone conveniently forgets who did what.

---

[6] *This information was taken from a blog by LA Weekly.*

Singer

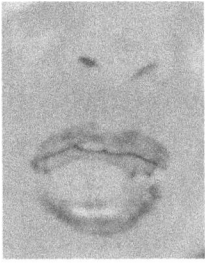

As a Singer you sing a Songwriter's songs.

You may be a Soloist, you may be in a Band or you may be a Theatrical/Operatic Performer.

Any aspiring Singer should have musical talent. The ability to work with people is necessary, especially if you are going to sing another person's work. You will need ambition and drive. You may feel that you can improve and hone your skill with vocal coaching. Vocal coaching can often extend your vocal range and possibly help you to learn new styles or languages. Interpretational ability or acting will be important, especially when performing a Songwriter's songs.

It is not imperative that you have professional training. Many Singers prefer to develop their own style. Depending on the genre of music that you intend to perform in, you will need to market and style yourself accordingly. Part of your marketing strategy should include promotional material (**EPK**). The EPK should incorporate a show reel (a CD or electronic MP3 featuring work that best shows off your voice), professional photographs, a biography (your Musical CV), any reviews you may have and links to your websites. Always ensure that your original material is properly protected before you send or hand out to a third party. You will find out how to do this in **Chapter 13, Copyright Protection**.

You may find it nerve-wracking when attending auditions for the first time. Provided these auditions are legitimate (see **Chapter 3, Performing Arts/X-Factor/Auditions**), these trials can give you experience and confidence. Some well-known performers have confessed to suffering from stage fright or getting audition nerves, even after many years of practice. Over time, it may be that auditions become few and far between as you successfully build your profile in your chosen field. Hopefully, the work will come to you instead of you having to go out and find it.

Management

You may feel as a Singer that being managed will help you handle your career and assist you in your search for work. Some Artists/Bands feel that Management can cause more headaches and problems, do little of the work required to promote their career and at a percentage cost to them, all before the Artist/Band has earned a bean. **BUT** if you are lucky to find Management who is **all singing and dancing**, has plenty of contacts, chaperones and protects you and your interests, then it could be worth forfeiting a percentage of your potential earnings.

However, if you are offered Management (or a Contract through an Agency) before you make a decision and sign off on a Contract, as with **ALL** contracts, do get a Solicitor to look over it. Some Management Contracts contain legally binding restrictions, whereby even if your Management no longer represents you, they are still entitled to a percentage of your earnings. This may be on a reducing percentage scale and can be up to a ten year period after termination, so it is imperative to read any Contract carefully.

Talking of the detail contained within a Contract, **Elvis Presley** clearly did not read the small print or was badly advised. His Manager, **Colonel Tom Parker** (who ironically was not a Colonel) took an astounding 50% (fifty per cent.) of **Elvis'** earnings towards the end of his career.[7]

Publishing

From a Publishing aspect, a Singer will have to agree to the terms of use as to whether **any** publishing will be received. Singers who sing another Songwriter's songs rarely receive publishing, unless the Singer is well-known (or established). Usually, this would be negotiated before any collaboration has taken place. If you are a Singer in a Band, then you are an integral part of the Group. However, you should never assume that you are entitled to a percentage of the Songwriting. Always insist on having an agreement in place from the outset so there can be no confusion at a later date.

As a Singer, whilst performing, you may come up with a hook or adlibs that recreate, shape or define a song. Many Singers have lost out financially and credibly because they have not believed **melisma** vital to the structure of the song. A Musician may deem a vocal performance inferior to the musical backing or a co-writer has refused to recognise vocal improvisation as part of the creative process during the writing of a song.

[7] *This information was taken from a blog by LA Weekly.*

One of the industry's best illustrations of this is the **Pink Floyd** track **The Great Gig in the Sky** from **The Dark Side of the Moon**.

The song was originally created by **Richard Wright**. Pink Floyd collectively tried a number of sounds, including NASA recordings of astronauts communicating on space missions, until finally Alan Parsons suggested they use the voice of **Clare Torry** who was a Session Singer at the time.

Torry gave a sterling performance and here we reach the **grey area**. **Torry** had not contributed lyrically and because she was paid a fee for her session work, **Torry** did not receive any mechanical royalty nor any publishing. Her vocal improvisation had shaped and defined the song thus giving her a **creative input**, but **Torry** only received her £30.00 session fee. Regardless of her great performance, **Pink Floyd** seemed underwhelmed and **Torry** left the Studio with the impression that her vocals would never make the final cut. **Torry** only realised that she was on the track when she saw the album at a local record shop and spotted her name in the credits.

In 2004, **Torry** sued **Pink Floyd** and **EMI** for songwriting royalties, on the basis that her contribution to the song constituted co-authorship with **Wright**. A settlement was reached in **Torry's** favour. All pressings after 2005 list the composition to **Wright** and **Torry**.[8]

If you are undecided and feel that you just want to **sing**, unsure if you can or even want to write songs, it is good to bear in mind that you can start out as a Singer, sing on a Songwriter's songs but as your career develops you may become categorised as a Singer then recommended for work **only** as a Singer thus making it extremely difficult for you to break free from that mantel.

Equally in today's industry, publishing now seems to be the **Golden Goose**. It seems most Songwriters, Producers and Record Labels will try their utmost to retain **any** and **all** share of the writing and publishing even if a Singer has helped shape the song.

---

[8] *This information was taken from an article in The Daily Express in 2004.*

Songwriter

My Song
by A Songwriter

Largo

If you cannot face the pomp and ceremony derived from being an Artist / Performer and only want to be a Songwriter, then you will have to get an Artist or a Band to record your songs.

Arguably, one of the most successful and best known American Songwriters is **Diane Warren**. **Warren** began songwriting in her early teens in the 1970s. Although coming from humble origins, **Warren's** insurance salesman Father backed her musical ambitions. He even opposed her Mother who tried to deter **Warren** by suggesting that she become a secretary.

Despite constant rejection, it took more than a decade before **Warren** was finally employed as a staff writer for **Laura Branigan's** producer **Jack White**. Since then **Warren's** songs have been performed by Artists such as **Aerosmith, Elton John, Tina Turner, Barbra Streisand, Aretha Franklin, Roberta Flack, Celine Dion, Whitney Houston, Roy Orbison, Eric Clapton, Lenny Kravitz, Pet Shop Boys, Joss Stone, Christina Aguilera, Enrique Iglesias, Jessica Simpson** and **Mary J. Blige**.

Regardless of her success, **Warren** is noted to be shy and uncomfortable in the limelight and has purposely remained behind the scenes, forfeiting the chance to be an Artist in her own right.

Management

If, as a Songwriter, you have signed a Management Contract then Management should help to pitch and promote your work.

Management should arrange collaborations and introduce new contacts, should you have need of co-writing partners. They should also deal with Publishing Companies, if you have agreed that they will attempt to attain a Publishing Contract for you.

Bear in mind that if Management arrange and are successful in getting you a Publishing Contract, Management will be entitled to their agreed percentage (i.e. 20%) of any advance offered. For instance, let us say that a Publishing Company is offering you a £25k advance upon future royalty, Management will be entitled 20% of £25k, a hefty £5,000 loss to you.

Effectively, if you do not want to shop around for a Publishing Contract and would prefer to have Management do this, then it is a fair exchange for payment of their services.

Publishing

From a publishing aspect, as a Songwriter, you are entitled to all (or a percentage of) the publishing (depending on whether you have written the song entirely alone or have collaborated with a co-writer). If you are a Composer of both music and vocal melody/lyrics, you own 100% (one hundred per cent.) of the publishing. However, if you co-wrote the song with another Songwriter, your percentage of the publishing will depend upon what has been agreed between you and your co-writer.

Session Singer/Musician

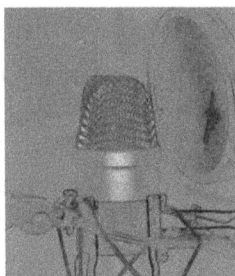

Session Singers/Musicians are instrumental and/or vocal performers covering all genres, that are available to work at live performances or recording sessions for a fee paid by the hour. While the fame and fortune of the big recording artists can be short-lived, Session Singers/Musicians can build a career lasting many years and often make a decent living. **BUT**, and this is a big deal, Session Singers/Musicians have to be professional. They have to arrive with all the equipment they need, in full working order and with a back-up in case of any eventuality and most importantly arrive punctually. There are no allowances for traffic, parking or broken down trains. They are paid to be ready to perform, exactly, first time, what is asked, in spite of any other factors.

Session Singers/Musicians are expected to learn parts quickly, read music and play by ear and tend to be used on a short-term basis. However, repeat gigs and tours are attainable, once a Session Singer/Musician has developed their reputation.

In 2011, BPI and the Musicians' Union entered into a new agreement for commissioning and paying UK session musicians. This agreement offers enhanced remuneration for session work and also greater flexibility to Record Labels, when making recordings using MU Session Singers/Musicians. Session Singers/Musicians and commissioning Record Labels will now sign a simple one-page **Session Agreement** for studio recordings or a **Live Recording Agreement** for concert recordings, accepting the terms of this new agreement. A standard audio session fee for a non-classical recording is **£120.00** or **£40.00** per hour.[9]

There is also an extra fee that can be agreed for overdubbing, doubling and trebling, anti-social hours, overtime and porterage. Session Singers/Musicians will receive a session fee, relevant additional fees, and a potential subsequent payment for each recording they perform on.

For more details about session work visit the MU website: http://www.musiciansunion.org.uk

It is well known that Session Singers/Musicians are some of the most talented musicians/singers in the industry and back in the 1950s most of the best known Artists may have started out as Session Musicians. So why is it, that in this day and age, they rarely rise to glory in their own right? I hazard a guess, personal choice and timing. From my time in the Music Industry, the overall consensus that I have experienced seems that in becoming a Session Singer/Musician, you are setting out your stall as an employee, someone that does not particularly crave centre stage. Yet to break free from the **gun for hire** mould can be a hard task. On the other hand, receiving a regular income, getting regular work, having a musical career with longevity, including the possibility of working with some of the biggest names in the industry offers a multitude of benefits.

The path of the Session Singer/Musician can be a great option if you want to get paid regularly and more importantly enjoy a varied and interesting career.

Management

As a Session Singer having Management will mean you are paying out a percentage, usually 20% (twenty per cent.) to someone to help you get work.

Alternatively, you can get yourself registered with a Session Agency. Session Agencies tend to find Singers and Musicians themselves and this is usually, **word of mouth**, based on a Singer/Musician's reputation, recommended to the Agency through their clients. Session Agencies will charge a booking fee. Again you need to be aware of empty promises tied up in a Contract, based on the premise of a 10-30% (ten to thirty per cent.) cut of your potential earning.

---

[9] *Subject to change, session fee rate as at December 2013*

Publishing

Because a fee is paid, most often Session Singers/Musicians will be required to sign a consent form, waiving their right to publishing royalties. In some cases, there may be negotiation for a percentage fee, if the Session Singer/Musician has had a significant involvement shaping the song (*see the case above re:* **Clare Torry** *on page 14*).

Changing Genre

Like most professions, a Singer/Songwriter's career is built upon experience and reputation. Similarly, when you change direction from one field of expertise to another, this may be met with scepticism. It seems the Music Industry is no different and does not like it when an Artist decides that they want to **change the goal posts**. For example, a **Country Singer** who wants to try their hand as a **Rap Artist**.

If after some time in your chosen genre, you have gained respect, work is flowing and your profile is peaking but as far as you are concerned **Jazz** is no longer for you. You feel you want to try to write and sing Country Songs instead. And while it may be something you feel compelled to do, nevertheless, do not be surprised if you are met with the **Snakes & Ladders** effect. Meaning, you find yourself back at the beginning or lower down your musical scale than before. Some known names have tried to cross into different genres, to find tough opposition from an already strong cast of established Artists. Despite being a well-known name in your own genre, because you have no reputation in this new field, you may be treated with contempt and more often with bewilderment.

Also, being an established name in one genre does not necessarily mean that you will cross over into your new genre at the same level. Unless your original genre fuses into the new category, you will be trying to attract new fans and possibly in the interim, alienating your original fan base, who may not like the new direction you are taking.

There is every chance you will have to build your profile from scratch in this new genre. You may have to start all over again. This does not mean that it cannot be done, nor should it put you off, but you may face opposition and criticism.

Frankly, I cannot see what is wrong with a bit of variety.

SYNOPSIS

Band Member: you prefer to work alongside people, but if you are not one of the Songwriters you may not receive any publishing royalty and should be aware of your rights.

Session Singer/Musician: you prefer to work behind the scenes helping other Artists with their songs and therefore are unlikely to receive any publishing royalty.

Singer: you sing someone else's songs and are therefore less likely to receive publishing royalty.

Singer/Songwriter: you write and sing your own songs. You retain all or a percentage of your publishing.

Songwriter: you write songs that someone else may record/perform. You retain all or a percentage of your publishing.

Do it yourself : How to get started

"Do not go where the path may lead, go instead where there is no path and leave a trail." (Ralph Waldo Emerson)

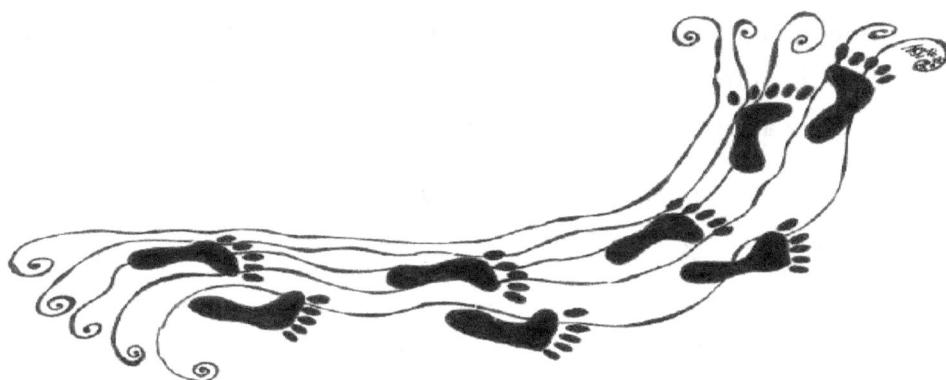

Like most careers, beginning is always the hardest part. Conquering your nerves, attaining *bona fide* introductions, overcoming false starts and dealing with time wasters are just a few of the many hurdles you may have to face.

The Music Industry is just like many other industries, in that its employers will want to know if you have any experience. They will want to see your musical curriculum vitae and hear about any of your accomplishments.

If you are not fortunate enough to have access to recording studio facilities, then getting yourself seen and heard can be nothing short of walking a minefield.

Before you can even start out on your path, you will need a good recording to **showcase** your voice and/or your songs. To do this, you will need access to recording equipment so that you can record yourself. If you do not have this kind of equipment or access to any equipment, you will need a contact with a recording studio or facilities who can record a show reel for you.

Without help or knowledge, it may seem like you are trapped in a never ending **catch 22** situation. With so many obstacles to overcome you may feel you just want to **give up**.

BUT DON'T!

Luckily, technology has moved on so far that most computers and even some mobiles phones have built in recording facilities. For example, **Apple Mac's Garageband** (which can be found on most **Apple Mac** computers including the **iPad**) is a great way to record a simple vocal or even to start creating your first song.

However, it is worth bearing in mind that the quality of recording on an iPad or a mobile phone is unlikely to be of industry standard, so you may still have to find another way to record your vocal/song.

It is understandable if you find the thought of using such technology yourself daunting.

Below are a few ideas which could help to get you started, without having to pay out any money on expensive equipment:

The Grapevine:

Ask around, somebody may know someone who has a home studio/recording studio who can help you. **BUT** be careful and **ALWAYS** take a chaperone when you attend even if you are visiting someone you know. Remember to leave the address where you are visiting with someone reliable.

Music Press:

NME/Local Paper/Loot/Free Ads – Bands often use these methods to advertise for a new Band Member. This may not help with recording your vocal / song but it could help with your confidence and give you experience. Preferably from a safety standpoint, most auditions should be held at a public venue but **NEVER** attend auditions or visit alone, always take someone with you. Leave details of where you are going with someone you can trust.

Music / Theatre Magazines:

Singer Magazine http://www.rhinegold.co.uk/magazines/the_singer/default.asp and **Equity** newsreel **The Stage** http://www.thestage.co.uk/. Equity is the Theatre Union assisting Actors and Performers principally. However, they are a great source of information. The Stage is filled with advertisements and opportunities from working at Butlins, situations on Cruises, to one day shoots where they need walk on actors/extras. Whilst some of these positions may only apply to Equity members or may not be the break you are looking for, it could give you some experience of auditions, knowledge of Agents, coaching, tuition and helpful advice. As always,

NEVER attend auditions or visit **ALONE**. Always take someone with you and leave the details and address of your audition with someone reliable.

Songwriting Services:

If you do not have any recording connections but have some savings there are several companies that offer Songwriting Services. These companies may help you record and formulate your song. Or if you do not have a song, they may be able to assist you to develop melody, lyrics, hooks and song structure. There are quite a few places who offer this kind of service and often they are attached to a Recording Studio. **CHECK** with them on **all** the costs before agreeing to anything.

NEVER visit **ALONE**. Always take someone with you as well as leaving details of where you are going with someone reliable.

Recording Studios:

If you have a song already prepared or if you are showcasing your voice, (for example, you may have a backing track of a known cover (i.e. *Falling into you - Celine Dion*) that you have purchased) then you can record your vocal at a Recording Studio. Check first with them regarding their fees. Some may charge by the hour or have hidden extras. **NEVER** attend **ALONE**. Have someone who is prepared to wait around with you. Also by having someone with you for support, may bolster your confidence if first recording nerves creep in. Leave the contact details and address of the Recording Studio with someone reliable. It would also be a good idea to let this person know your timings, as you may be there sometime, especially if you are planning to record one of your own songs.

Home Recording:

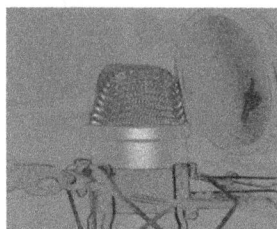

If you have savings then it may be a good idea to invest in a home studio. I have worked out of a home studio for the past decade. Thanks to the internet, I liaise with my co-writers by email, record my work in my studio and then send over my dry vocals and songs without having to open my front door.

Take some time to research products. There are many variations available. Your local college may run a course for engineering/recording so you can get first-hand knowledge of the product you intend to use.

Deciding whether you are going to work on a MAC or a PC will determine what software you will be able to use.

If you are a MAC user, by visiting your local Apple Store you may be able to get a demonstration of their products.

It is often debated which recording product is better, **Logic** or **Cubase**. Both systems have been updated and improved extensively. At the last innings, Cubase was edging slightly ahead due to a wide spectrum of functionality.

Both of these products are used by industry professionals.

So, it really comes down to whether you prefer working on a PC or a MAC.

Logic Pro is a digital audio workstation with MIDI sequencer software used alongside an Apple Mac computer.

For specifications visit the website at: http://www.apple.com/uk/logic-pro/

Logic Express is a simplified version that works in conjunction with Apple products.

Both of these are available through the Apple Store.

If you prefer to work on a PC then you may be able to get hold of an old version of Logic. Versions up to version 5.5 may work on a PC but anything after Logic 5 will be for **MAC users only**.

◀⊙ CUBASE

Cubase is a music software product developed by German musical software and equipment company Steinberg for music digital recording, arranging and editing.

For specifications see their website at:

http://www.steinberg.net/en/products/cubase/start.html.

Cubase can be used with either a PC or MAC.

If you are a Singer/Songwriter, it is worth investing in a good mic. You do not have to spend thousands of pounds and often suppliers may have deals on some of their stock so it is worth shopping around. Again, check forums and reviews to see which is the best product for you.

Performing Arts / X-Factor / Auditions

"Music hath charms to sooth a savage breast, to soften rocks, or bend a knotted oak." (William Congreve – The Mourning Bride)

It seems that more and more Performing Arts Schools, Theatrical Colleges, Stage/Drama Schools and Agencies are opening up, highlighting the steady increase in the demand for new talent. Most of these establishments run a cornucopia of courses, catering from TV Hosting, Acting, Dance and Performance, Studio Engineers to Stage Designers.

They will train, define and help you to perfect your talent, augmenting invaluable knowledge and if you want a career in the theatre, film or television this is really the best path to follow. As a Singer or Singer/Songwriter there may be less to gain from attending one of these institutions. In that they will train you a certain way, which, as an original Artist could be conflicting, nevertheless the experience gained and possible contacts to be made can only enhance your success.

It seems over the past ten to fifteen years, more of these schools are catering to the Music Industry. They coach and groom prospective stars for their clients that may include A&R representation from Major Record Labels.

So there is always a chance that they could start you on the road to glory. With all things, there is no definite formula or guarantee for assured success. Not every person attending a Performing Arts School will go on to be massively successful, but it is certainly an avenue to think about.

Performing Arts Schools

There are a host of Performing Arts Schools in the UK but below I have listed three of the most well-known establishments.

The Italia Conti Academy of Theatre Arts

The Italia Conti Academy of Theatre Arts (http://www.italiaconti.com) is the oldest theatre arts training school in the world. The school was developed when **Italia Conti**, an established Actress, was invited by the Producer, **Charles Hawtrey** to teach children for his first production of **Where the Rainbow Ends** which opened at the Savoy Theatre, London in 1911.

These days the Academy offers a full range of courses (including short courses) for performing arts, held at its numerous associate school branches found throughout the Country.

The Academy award a limited number of Scholarships for full-time and short course training annually. The scholarships vary in value and are always for tuition fees only.

As an established bastion, the Academy is frequently invited by the theatrical profession to appear at events. Many of their students have performed in numerous functions from the Royal Variety, Her Majesty Queen Elizabeth's 40th Anniversary and Golden Jubilee Anniversary Celebrations to The Children In Need Appeals for BBC Television.

The Brit School

The London School for Performing Arts & Technology (or **The BRIT School**) is located in Selhurst, Croydon.

It provides training for the performing arts, media, art and design (http://www.brit.croydon.sch.uk) and is notable for its famous alumni including **Katy B**, **Adele**, **Amy Winehouse**, **Jessie J**, **Leona Lewis**, **Katie Melua**, **The Kooks**, **Kate Nash** and **The Feeling** and many more.

The Brit School is Government funded with support from the British Record Industry Trust. This helps it maintain independent school status from the local education authority and is remarkably, one of the only performing arts schools in the country that is still free to attend.

Although, not a surety, it seems the Music Industry **cherry picks** from the school making it high on the list for would be pop stars.

The Sylvia Young Theatre School

The Sylvia Young Theatre School, is predominantly known for musical theatre/performing arts (http://www.sylviayoungtheatreschool.co.uk). However, it was home to **Emma Bunton**, **Billie Piper** and **Amy Winehouse** at one time.

With term fees of over £10,000 a year, this route is one to take if you have financial backing or are lucky enough to attain a full scholarship through The Andrew Lloyd Webber Foundation.

The X Factor

Unless you have lived under a rock for many years, you will have some inkling of **The X Factor**.

The X Factor is a television music competition set out to find new singing talent. Prospective hopefuls attend public auditions (http://xfactor.itv.com). The overall winner goes onto receive a £1 million Recording Contract with Record Label **Syco Music**. This includes a cash payment to the winner, but note, the majority is allocated to marketing and recording costs.

It seems a sure-fire way of becoming a megastar. Recently several well-known Musicians/Artists have spoken out publicly against such shows. Stating that in their view, entry into the profession this way was a **cop out**, relaying that their idols such as **Elvis, Jim Morrison, Kate Bush, Joni Mitchell** et al would never have been discovered by a singing contest. Whichever way you look at it, discovery through the **media** was and still is commonplace. In the 1950s, a lot of the stars of that era were picked out from local competitions.

Like any profession, it really depends how **YOU** want to be viewed.

If you want global domination and are prepared to slog it out, long and hard, through copious auditions, forsaking some of your ideals (including Songwriting) then one of these contests could fast forward your career.

But if you see yourself as an original Artist then perhaps the above direction would not suit you. You may prefer taking the **tried and tested** route (see **Chapter 6, Tried and Tested**) to see what the hand of fate deals you.

Auditions and Song Competitions

On your search for success, you may come across advertisements for competitions, sent directly to you by email or posted on the internet on a social networking website.

I am always very wary of so-called competitions. In my experience, most of these come to naught and tend to want to charge you something just for the privilege of entering.

Unless a Songwriting or Singing Competition is fully backed by a *bona fide* Radio Station, Television or a known company, along with genuine entrance applications, I would hazard a guess that it will be a money spinner and not genuine.

For example, one known internet company charge a $45 fee per entry, per song. They invite Artists/Bands to send in songs electronically, on the enticement that they may be selected to play at big concerts, festivals or attain that all-enticing Record Deal. However, a few years ago the Showcase Director from this company forwarded an email in error asking over **650 bands** to let him know which days they might be able to play.

About an hour later, the same 650 bands received an email saying the following:

"There is a bug in our system and the wrong email was sent out to many people.
Sorry for any inconvenience this may have caused.

This is the email that you should have received:

It is with regret that we inform you we are unable to find a slot for you to perform at the ABC Music Venue."

With over 650 bands paying $45.00 per entry, this Company was making a whopping **$30k** just from one competition. To add insult to injury, none of the bands even got an audition, concluding that these operations are nothing more than money making **scams**, that can generate millions at the expense of the Artists and Bands who pay their imaginary subscription fees.

Your Career : Getting Support

"Action is the foundational key to all success." (Pablo Picasso)

S tatistics show, that only a small minority of published Songwriters make enough money every year to be able to dedicate to Songwriting full-time, without the subsidy of a second income. Despite the cloudy outlook, remember, it only takes **one song** to change your life and despite the low chances of success, for many Songwriters, it is those who **kept at it** that went on to succeed.

So, if you are serious about being a Songwriter, then there is one important thing to remember. This is **YOUR** career and **YOU** need to be happy with the choices you are making or being asked to make.

The path of a Singer/Songwriter can sometimes be a very solitary one. When reading from one of the many performer biographies, often they touch upon aspects of loneliness at the top. But not everyone experiences isolation and perhaps you will be fortunate and find yourself surrounded by people that care and look out for you.

Either way, rejection and learning to deal with rejection will either come naturally or be something you will have to learn. To bounce back, despite proverbial doors being shut in your face requires a dogged determination and the main attribute to Pop star/Artist/Actor success. A quote, which has stayed with me and has helped me through some difficult moments in my career:

"winners are just losers who never gave up"

Obviously there has to come a time when perhaps you need to reassess your career. It is at these times, that you need to be honest with yourself and set some ground rules:

*what you **want** to accomplish*

*what you **will do** to achieve it*

*what you **will not do** in order to achieve it*

You may have heard the old adage:

"It's about being at the right place, at the right time"

I believe life and career is always about timing. For me, most of the times when I could have really pushed my career forward I skipped out. This was purely a personal choice but it was **MY** choice and something I would not change.

When I look back at my career, the triumphs, successes and failures, for me the main bone of contention was always during the low points, when I felt undervalued and overlooked. I evaluated my career against my contemporaries.

Over time, a valuable lesson has been learned.

It is far too easy to judge yourself against the accomplishments of your peers. Those who have already established themselves amongst the higher echelons of the Music Industry. Firstly, you have no idea what they have undertaken on their journey to attain such fame. Secondly, signing ones soul over to the Devil just isn't for everyone.

Joining the MU and/or other Societies may offer you career opportunities through their community but in truth, your career will only take you so far as you want it to.

"when it comes to your career, be active, not inactive"

If you want people to recognise your work then you need to be committed and active.

You have to use whatever media and services are available to you.

Most importantly you should protect yourself and use the media you are most comfortable with.

Promotion

There are many different ways for you to help yourself get noticed. Below are some of the most common ways using Social Media:

Twitter: www.twitter.com is a social networking and microblogging website enabling users to send "tweets" text-based posts of up to 140 characters. Use this to promote your work, build a fanbase and raise your profile.

Myspace: www.myspace.com is a social networking website with over 25 million users. Lily Allen and Kate Nash both found fame through Myspace. Not as popular as before but you can still use this to promote your work, build a fanbase and raise your profile.

Facebook: www.facebook.com is a social networking website with over 25 million users. You can have fan pages as well as your own page/band pages with **follow** or **like** options allowing you to have as many fans as possible. Artists and fans can interact via Facebook.

see me: www.see.me is a website where you can share your creative work and get recognised. They estimate a global community of over 650,000 creatives.

tumblr: www.tumblr.com is a microblogging platform and social networking website allowing users to post multimedia and other content to a short-form blog. You can post text, photos, links, music and videos from wherever you happen to be.

YouTube: www.youtube.com a website where you can share your videos and music and also earn money. Justin Beiber was discovered and found international fame through Youtube.

Soundcloud: www.soundcloud.com is a website that provides a place for musicians to showcase their work, allows collaboration, promotion and distribution of audio recordings without having a record deal.

Reverbnation: www.reverbnation.com is a website that provides a place for musicians, producers and venues to communicate.

Yahoo: www.yahoo.co.uk/com best known as a search engine, Directory, Mail, News, Groups, video sharing, social networking media website and services. Use their free email to connect and promote yourself.

Google: www.google.com a web portal, search engine, directory, with free mail and services. Google alert helps you keep track of news about topics you are interested in, you can also use it to alert you about you and your work. Google+ is a social networking element that helps you promote and connect with fans and collaborators.

Instagram: http://instagram.com/# is a free site where you can upload photos and videos to share your life with friends, family and fans.

Websites: there are a multitude of companies out there who offer do-it-yourself web design and web building and a lot of these are free. Some may charge a small yearly fee for hosting but these days there is no excuse not to have your own website as most of them are easy to use, include designer made templates, hosting, innovative Apps and features for free so you do not have to pay a web developer/designer.

No doubt, more social media sites will come to light after this book goes into publication, so you will need to keep abreast of what the Industry is leaning towards.

Part of being an Artist is thinking of new and innovative ways to get your music heard and yourself noticed. However, as I mentioned above, it is important to correctly use the media you feel comfortable with. There are provisions in place with most of the above websites to protect your identity while you build your fan base.

Remember, it is great to interact with your audience, to get attention, but you do not need to give them every bit of information about yourself. Besides, a bit of mystery is far more tantalising.

I cannot stress this next point enough.

Even if there is a chance you may get work, **NEVER** post your telephone, mobile or address publicly, **anywhere**.

Create an internet address and direct all prospective clients to that address. And if at any time, you feel you are being pressured or bullied, these sites have parameters set in place to protect you.

Networking through Associations

There are many Associations you can join that will offer networking and work opportunities. I have found most of them charge a fee.

Musicians' Union (MU)

**Musicians'
Union**

mu   http://www.musiciansunion.org.uk

If you intend to perform live on a regular basis then I would recommend joining the Musicians' Union. As well as their legal liability there are many benefits to MU membership which include:

Insurance/Pension/Tax Advice

Members are insured for legal liability of £10m, to cover injury to members of the public or damage to property and instrument/equipment insurance up to £2,000. Personal Accident cover and tax investigation cover and access to Professional Indemnity Insurance Scheme. The MU offers a Tax Saving Guide and advice on Pension schemes.

Legal Advice

There is a free Legal Service for all members from dealing with disputes for unpaid fees, cancellations, injury compensation, intellectual property rights to advice on contracts for recording, songwriting, touring or merchandising.

Nationwide Networking

The MU has an online noticeboard so you can network with fellow musicians. There are dedicated helplines for personal, legal, financial and medical assistance and access to music–focused and other courses and workshops.

Rights Protection

The MU offers protection for your copyright and property rights and they are continually updating rights' service for musicians in recording and publishing, including online developments.

Teacher Services

If you are a Music Teacher, the MU offers assistance with lesson planning documentation, obtaining Criminal Records Bureau clearance, National Insurance contributions, pension issues, claiming holiday pay and other teaching-related matters.

Courses/Seminars/Workshops

The MU runs courses and workshops throughout the year, across the UK, where industry professionals give advice to Members.

The British Academy of Songwriters, Composers and Authors (BASCA)

The voice for music writers   http://www.basca.org.uk/

BASCA campaigns in the UK, Europe and throughout the world. BASCA is well known for putting on the British Composer Awards, the Gold Badge Awards and The Ivors every year. They are an independent, self-funding professional association representing music writers in all genres, from songwriting, through to media, contemporary classical and jazz.

BASCA was formed over 65 years ago and its members include Sir Paul McCartney, Dizzee Rascal, Michael Nyman, Gary Barlow, David Arnold, Sir Elton John, Imogen Heap, Kate Bush, Chris Martin, amongst others.

BASCA's mission statement:

BASCA exists to support and protect the artistic, professional, commercial and copyright interests of Songwriters, Lyricists and Composers of all genres of music and to celebrate and encourage excellence in British music writing.

Professional Membership : To be eligible for Professional Membership of BASCA, you must be a Full or Associate member of PRS for Music or have equivalent status within an overseas collection society.

Standard Membership : To be eligible for Standard Membership of BASCA, you must be a Provisional member of PRS for Music or have equivalent status within an overseas collection society.

Student Membership : Student Membership is open to any music writer who is over 18 years of age and currently in full time higher education, regardless of the course you are studying. Student membership is capped at three years.

Incorporated Society of Musicians (ISM)

ISM
INCORPORATED SOCIETY OF | MUSICIANS   http://www.ism.org/

The Incorporated Society of Musicians (**ISM**) is a professional body for musicians in the UK. You are eligible to join if you are working as a professional within music. As a member you have access to:

Legal Support
One-to-one legal advice on contracts, IP, employment.
24-hour legal helpline.
Legal expenses cover for up to £100,000 of legal costs
Standard contracts and agreements
Fee recovery service

Insurance
Public liability insurance - £10 million of essential cover
Employers' liability insurance - £10 million
Professional indemnity insurance
Discounts of 10-20% off musical instrument insurance

Tax Support
24-hour tax helpline
Tax return completion service

Tax investigation cover - your accountant's fees are covered if you have an HMRC investigation of your personal tax affairs

Expert Advice
Guidance Documents
One-to-one advice from ISM staff
Fees surveys and recommendations

Personal and Wellbeing Advice
Advice on managing your personal finances
Access to 24-hour telephone counselling
Advice on health and lifestyle issues affecting musicians

Promotion and Professional Development
Create your own ISM profile
Use of the ISM member logo
Promote your events on our website and social media pages
Professional development programme
National conferences
Events at local ISM venues
Online community

News and Exclusive Offers
Magazine
Member's Handbook
Discounts

Featured Artists Coalition (FAC)

http://www.thefac.org/

The FAC is a non-profit organisation formed in March 2009. Funded by contributions it has one full-time staff member. There is no fee to join but you can make an optional donation.

The FAC represents the interests of **Featured Artists** (performers that are generally considered to form a Band (i.e. the individuals that make up **Radiohead**) or that are understood to be a Singer/Solo Performer (i.e. **Annie Lennox**)) within the national and European political arenas on issues such as copyright law, music licensing working closely with the

MMF and the MU on legislative and policy issues. They offer a number of services including, connecting artists with companies and other artists, help and advice on new technologies and negotiations with companies to secure favourable terms for all FAC artists.

The FAC's Board of Directors are a list of who's who in the Music Industry including: **Kate Nash**, **Ed O'Brien**, **Dave Rowntree**, **Howard Jones**, **Sandie Shaw**, **Annie Lennox** and **Fran Healy**.

The International Songwriters Association (ISA)

http://www.songwriter.co.uk

The ISA was founded in 1967. Members receive Songwriter Magazine, Songwriter Update, and Songwriter Newsflash and have free ISA Services as Song Copyright, Song Assessment, Advice and Directory Information. On joining you receive an ISA Members Package which includes the Songwriter Yearbook and access to the ISA Private Members Site which has hundreds of articles, interviews, back issues of all publications, a notice board, tip sheet, videos, directories etc. Unfortunately, you cannot join the ISA as they are over-subscribed but their website is worth a visit for information.

LINKEDIN

http://uk.linkedin.com/

LinkedIn is a large professional network with 200 million members in 200 countries and territories around the globe.

LinkedIn takes your professional network online to give you access to people, jobs and opportunities. With currently more than 200 million professionals including executives, from all five hundred of the Fortune

500 companies, as well as a wide range of household names in technology, financial services, media, consumer packaged goods, entertainment, and numerous other industries.

SKYPE

http://www.skype.com/en/

Skype is a service that you can use if you prefer to negotiate and talk to people. You can use it for voice (telephone / mobile) and video calls, instant messaging and file sharing to anyone who is on Skype.

However, as with any telephone call, face to face meeting or discussion, unless you record your conversations (which you would have to disclose to the other participant(s) that this was your intention, before you commenced recording the conversation) there will be no record of what you have agreed.

Although oral (gentlemen's agreements) arrangements are legally binding, they can be difficult to prove further along the collaboration process. Rather than get into a **he said/she said** scenario, it is always best to follow up all telecons (calls or meetings on the telephone) with confirmatory emails, setting out the details and terms you have agreed in the conversation.

Even better, follow up with a Contract setting out those established provisions.

Tried and Tested

"There is only one way a band can function......and that's on the bloody stage" (Robert Plant, Led Zeppelin)

Over the past fifty years or so, the **tried and tested** route to musical stardom was to get out on tour and gig. Some of the biggest and most well-known Bands and Artists have spent years (in some cases most of their musical career) on the road and many of those Bands have returned to touring time and time again, because it became a way of life.

Live performances and going on tour is still regarded by many as the best route to follow. One way to describe it would be like doing work experience. The more work experience you get, so your artistry is honed and perfected and with the rebirth of the Festival there are even more opportunities to perform live. This means, not only will your fans get to see you, but there is always the chance that there may be an A&R Representative in the audience, waiting to sign you, off the back of your performance.

The Music Industry is a small pond. If people are coming to see you, the chances are they are talking about you, recommending you to their friends and posting about you on social media sites. This kind of exposure may give an A&R Representative for a

Record Label, the **heads up** about you, possibly encouraging them to show their interest by coming to see you at your next gig.

If you are just starting out, then arranging a mini-tour yourself and inviting Record Labels to your performances is another great way of being seen by the right people.

Another benefit of gigging and touring is building that all-important fan base. To be seen performing live on stage is probably one of the best ways to interact with your fans and pick up prospective new fans. Promoting the gig afterwards, sharing news, creating a blog, posting photos are all ways to share and involve your fans further. You may find that your fan base increases with each performance.

Handing out flyers with your website and contact details is a prudent way of making sure important people can always contact you. It also means that you never miss any opportunity, including interest from a Record Label.

However, do not assume that the **tried and tested** route will bring you overnight fame. For instance, it took the **Goo Goo Dolls** over ten years of hard touring before they finally achieved recognition.

The **Goo Goo Dolls** single "**Name**" became a Top 10 in the US propelling their fifth studio album "**A Boy Named Goo**" into gold-record sales.

> *"It means being willing to have one day off in six months and then have somebody call you and say, 'I need you to do this for me' and doing it, it's being willing not to make a penny when everybody around you is making money and all your friends are finishing grad school and stuff and you're out in a van."*[10]

---

[10] *LA Times November 18, 1995 Richard Cromelin quoting John Rzeznik of the Goo Goo Dolls.*

Record Labels

"The music business is a cruel and shallow money trench. A long plastic hallway where pimps and thieves run free and good men die like dogs. There is also a negative side." (Hunter S. Thompson)

What springs to mind, when you think of a Record Label? Something exciting and glamorous?

However the Record Label of today is very different from those of yesteryear and thanks to the Digital Age, anyone can set up a website and call themselves a Record Label.

What is a Record Label?

Ironically the term **Record Label** originates from the round label in the middle of a vinyl record on which the Record Company name, along with the artist, song title and other information would have been printed. Today, due to costs, very few **Vinyl Records** are pressed, although the title Record Label still exists.

Record Labels come in all shapes and sizes. The three major Record Labels are conglomerates who own a variety of other Record Labels. If you imagine an umbrella with the finial, at the top, being the Parent Company, below it are the Subsidiaries, smaller Record Labels. These smaller Record Labels tend to specialise, often operating as a separate entity.

Most Record Labels function in more or less same fundamental way. Depending on the size of a Record Label will determine whether they can afford sections to categorise and separate the areas of work and development.

If you are signed to a Major Record Label there is every chance that you or your Management will have dealings with some of the following divisions within the company:

A&R

You may have come across the term **A&R**.

Artists and Repertoire (**A&R**) is the arm of a Record Label that is responsible for finding new Artists and Acts for their company. Effectively, they are talent scouts. Yesteryear, they would have visited venues and contests to sign an Artist/Band on the back of a performance.

However, A&R's key role today is the search for the next big hit. This usually means sifting through tracks to see which, if any, have potential, liaising with Songwriters to write Toplines for their Artist's or arranging Producers and studio time. In Major and Large / Medium Record Labels an A&R Representative may also have to deal with overseeing the artistic development of a newly signed recording Artist/Band, acting as a liaison between the Artist/Band and the Record Label.

Art Department

Some corporations have an Art Department. An Art Department is responsible for the design of an Artist/Band's single and album covers, advertisements, tour merchandise and website artwork. Basically they design anything used to promote both tangibly and digitally.

Accounts

Most Record Labels should account to you with bi-annual statements.

These statements should list the track (or tracks) you have signed to the Record Label. If they have given you an advance fee, this fee will be deducted before you receive any royalty from them.

Development

Artist Development is the department that works with a Band or an Artist to help with career decisions.

Distribution /Label Liaison

Often, Record Labels use a separate Distribution Company but the Major Record Labels may still have a branch called **Label Liaison.** This division is essentially the people who get your music where it needs to be, acting as the link between the Record Label and the Distributor.

Legal

The Legal Department is one of the key departments in a Major Record Label. Record Labels and entertainment Solicitors/Lawyers go hand in hand and seemingly one cannot exist without the other because fundamentally this is where the **deals are sealed**.

Most legal issues will be dealt with by either in-house Solicitor or a Law Firm hired by the Record Label.

Marketing

The Marketing Team of a Major Record Label has to coordinate a marketing plan ensuring the utmost exposure for an Artist/Band. It is their job to guarantee that the paying public gets to see and hear the Artist/Band and their music.

New Media

The prolific New Media field encompasses the role of relentless and instant access to content on any digital device. They act as a link to streaming an Artist's/Band's work, video promotion, user participation and creative feedback via the internet.

Promotion/PR (Public Relations)

Promotion and PR work may be outsourced to a Promotion/PR specialist. This includes **Pluggers** who will **test the water** on an Artist's/Band's track. A Report is usually sent out to Radio and Club DJs using a marking system with comment sections enabling the DJs to confirm whether they intend to support the track.

The main objective of Promotion/PR is to ensure Radio, TV and video airplay and to expose the Artist/Band to every aspect of media from Radio, TV and magazines.

Sales Team

Any large Company will have some kind of sales team selling their Product to the general consumer and a Major Record Label is no different.

What does a Record Label do?

A Record Label signs and develops an Artist/Band. If the Artist/Band is just starting out, they may arrange for the Artist/Band to record their song(s). The song(s) will then become the **Master Recording** which in turn shall be distributed either territorially or globally. The size of the Record Label will ascertain as to how much time and finance is invested in the Artist/Band and the music. With a Major Record Label, because they may have in-house resources, this could ensure that an Artist/Band achieves earlier recognition.

What is Licensing?

If an Artist has signed a track or an album to a Record Label, it is quite common that the Recording Contract will contain a provision that sets out the details for Licensing. This means that the Record Label can sell your track or album to another company to distribute (sell) your track or album in the agreed territory(ies).

If your Record Label is based in the UK but they have licensed your track to a company in New Zealand for onward distribution in Australasia, then they have the right to sell your work in that territory (Australasia)).

Your Record Label would normally receive a fee. Depending on your Contract, you may or may not be entitled to some of that fee in royalties. In a standard Licensing Contract, if the Company that your Record Label licensed your work to makes a profit selling your work in the territory, they keep all that profit and you will not receive any mechanical royalty, beyond what is stipulated in your original Contract.

But, if your Record Label signs a Licensing Contract ensuring that Company takes all the risk and your work produces no distribution profit but instead makes a deficit, this will not have any financial impact on your Record Label or (more importantly) you.

What is Distribution?

Distribution refers to getting your singles, EPs and albums into the shops and onto the internet. If you are signed to a Major Record Label they will have an in-house Distributor or an affiliate that they use.

A smaller Record Label that has signed a distribution deal will only make money on goods that have been sold. Usually a distribution deal will mean that the Record Label is responsible for manufacturing and promotion. This means if the Product makes a lot of money, they will keep a large percentage (in some cases all gross proceeds) but if the Product sits on the shelves, the Record Label could lose money which effectively will come out of your mechanical royalty.

Types of Record Label

There are a multitude of Record Labels, listed globally and covering every genre. To simplify, it can be broken into three categories:

Major Record Label (including Sub-Labels)

Genre Based / Vanity / Boutique Record Labels

Small / Independent Record Labels

Record Labels come in all shapes and sizes from **Small, Independent** ("**Indie**") or **Major** (as part of a large Media Group).

Major Record Label

Since the late 19th century and the invention of the Gramophone by **Emile Berliner** so recording on flat disks (**records)** was created and the Record Label was born. **Columbia Records** was one of the first Major Record Labels and like so many others who have come and gone before them, **Columbia** is now owned by a larger company, **Sony Music Entertainment**. As of 2012 there were only three labels that are referred to as a "**Major Record Label**".

The three Major Record Labels (International Media groups) are:

Sony Music Entertainment

Warner Music Group

Universal Music Group

Together these Major Record Labels control a large percentage of the market

The main difference between a Major Record Label and other Record Labels is that a Major Record Label owns its own distribution channel. Major Record Labels are multi-national companies that collectively account for a much bigger percentage of record and music video sales across the world market.

Sub-Labels

A **Sub-Label** is a Record Label that is part of a larger Company and trades under a different name from their Parent Company, i.e. **Siren Records** is a Sub-Label of **Capital Music Group** who are owned by **Universal**, a Major Record Label.

When a Record Label is not a Company (i.e. without a legal business structure) it is usually called an **imprint** which can be marketed as **project**, **unit**, or **division** of the Record Label:

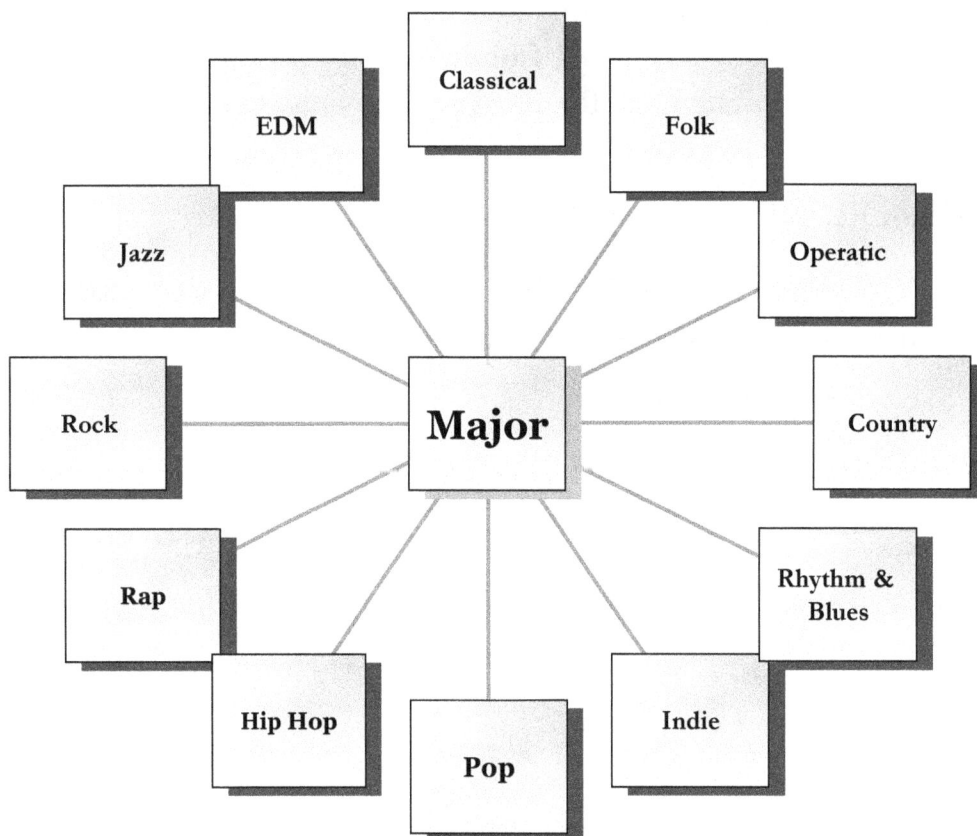

Genre Based /Vanity / Boutique Record Labels

Vanity Labels are Record Labels that suggest an Artist/Band owns it or has some control of its day to day running. This association remains within the typical margins of a Record Label and Artist/Band set up but with the exception that this kind of relationship often lends the Artist/Band more creative freedom and input towards their career.

For example, Record Labels within the **EDM (Electronic Dance Music)** genre are usually fronted by a big named DJ/Artist like **Armin van Buuren (Armada)** or **Tiesto (Black Hole Recordings**[11]).

Where Major Record Labels have financial backing to cross genres, these Record Labels tend to specialise in one genre, or in genres that fuse or overlap i.e. Trance and House or EDM collectively.

Independent Record Label

A few examples of Independent Record Labels:

Often Independent Record Labels do not have the financial backing and resources of the Major Record Labels. However, some Independent Record Labels have become

---

[11] *Tiesto left Black Hole Recordings to start a new Label Musical Freedom in association with PLAS Entertainment Group in 2010.*

so successful that a Major Record Label has entered into a distribution agreement for the music signed to that Record Label.

Sometimes, a Major Record Label buys shares in an Independent Record Label in order to attain control. If a Major Record Label owns 50% or more of the total shares in an Independent Record Label, there is every chance that Record Label will then be controlled by the Major Record Label and little or no control will be left with the Independent Record Label. There have even been some cases where a Major Record Label has bought an Independent Record Label in its entirety.

Whilst, it is easy to believe that signing a big record deal with a Major Record Label will be the best way forward, do not overlook the Small and Independent Record Labels. Firstly, they may be more open to signing you on your terms and with less restriction. Secondly, a lot of the Small and Independent Record Labels are creative and musical pioneers who have played a massive part within the Music Industry, breaking acts like **Oasis** and **Björk**.

It is worth noting that, some of the Independent Record Labels have been around for many years, establishing their stronghold within the profession, creating music scenes and making music history.

Digital Record Label

These days anyone can set up a Digital Record Label.

New Digital Record Labels appear weekly and can be created by anyone, of any age, with or without experience and specialising in any genre. Unfortunately, because these Digital Record Labels cost little to create and have minimal yearly maintenance, they can be up and running in a matter of days.

If you have been offered a deal with a Digital Record Label, there are a few things to bear in mind.

First, you will need to check that their Recording Contract contains provisions that protect and account to you correctly.

Second, before you sign their Recording Contract it would be prudent to ascertain exactly how they intend to promote and market your music.

Some Digital Record Labels will not invest in you as an Artist/Band nor will they have any intention of financing the promotion of your work. They may have little or no knowledge of the industry in your genre and if they are not an already established source they may rely on you to provide a fan base or database of contacts which will only be of benefit to them.

Being signed by a Record Label?

To some Artists/Bands, the idea of being signed by a Record Label is their life ambition. Many are of the opinion that by signing a Recording Contract and getting a **Record Deal,** their life will change overnight.

Unless you sign to a Major Record Label, sale of a tangible distribution to your fan base or a target audience may elude you. This is because it is quite usual for some Record Labels to offer only the link to a website where prospective purchasers can download an MP3.

Theoretically, Record Labels should take time and possibly invest money into the promotion and marketing of the work of an Artist/Band, so that the work reaches its audience. However, it may be that the Record Label takes the stance of offering just the MP3 link, which may mean that your song sells few copies. This leaves you with the task of self-promoting, **spamming**, through social media websites in the hope that you reach your target audience and fan base thereby enabling them to purchase your songs.

Today, signing a Contract with a Record Label differs from Label to Label. It will also depend on how high up the **music / commercial food chain** you are. Recently, the term (the length of time (years) you are contracted to that Record Label) seems to have increased from five years to ten years. In many cases some Record Labels are placing the term **in perpetuity** (forever) in their contracts due to the growing need for the retention of copyright. This means that the Record Label can continue to earn from your work through back catalogues and licensing indefinitely.

On a positive note, **the public gets what the public wants**. They get to see their favourite Artist/Band without any real notion of what goes on behind the scenes. None of this would be possible without a good team working on their behalf.

Renowned for his anti-corporation views, **Neil Young**, took a media conference by surprise when he commented in an interview:

"What I like about record companies is that they present and nurture artists. That doesn't exist on iTunes, it doesn't exist on Amazon. That's what a record company does, and that's why I like my

record company. People look at record companies like they're obsolete, but there's a lot of soul in there – a lot of people who care about music, and that's very important."[12]

What is a Recording Contract?

A Recording Contract is an Agreement that legally binds an Artist/Band to a Record Label. Most reputable Record Labels will offer a reasonable and fair contract. Many EDM Record Labels will sign an Artist/Band on a track per track basis. On occasion these Record Labels may set a provision in place, an option for a second track, based on the success of the first track. Basically, Record Labels will only sign Artist's/Band's or Tracks they feel will sell because they are a business and want to make money.

What is a Master Recording?

The copyright for a Master Recording is owned by the person who made the recording. Typically this is the Artist/Band (or in some cases a Producer and the Artist jointly). Unless an Artist/Band has assigned their rights in the Master Recording to a Record Label, the Artist/Band may claim ownership interest in a Master Recording.

In earlier years, a Record Label would automatically own the Master Recording because it would have organised its creation. This is no longer the case, unless they have arranged for the Artist/Band to record the work or if the Artist/Band has assigned this right over to them, but this would usually be set out within a Record Contract.

---

[12] *This information was taken from The Guardian Music Blog in an article by Helienne Lindvall on 2 February 2012.*

Management

It is smal reason you should kepe a dog, and barke your selfe
(Brian Melbancke - Philotimus: the Warre Betwixt Nature and
Fortune)

Managers have the ability to propel their client onto the music scene, steering them and shaping them so that they reach the heady heights of stardom and cavernous wealth. Equally, there is always a flipside and many an Artist/Band has been manacled in a deal, where their creativity is impeded and/or they have received little or no financial reward, all due to lack of work or crippling arrangements that limit and obstruct any productive process.

Dream Team or Fall Guy?

Management and Artist/Band are a team. As a team neither will function properly if the other does not perform to the agreed target, clarified in a Management Contract previously agreed to by all Parties.

Management must fulfil the needs of the Artist/Band. Management should take the strain of the business upon their shoulders, leaving the Artist/Band free, uninhibited and able to create their work.

The Artist/Band must fulfil their role as the creative. To perform, show up when required and behave in a manner acceptable to their agreement.

Both Management and Artist/Band need characteristics suitable to their respective roles. This successful espousement helps attain a common objective.

If the mechanics of either role become confused, then a strain is put on the relationship. For example, if Management talks about another Artist/Band they also manage, ignoring client requests or if an Artist/Band refuses to turn up to the studio to record and/or behaves inappropriately. Any one of these scenarios may lead to a situation where either party is in breach of contract and ultimately they could decide to go their separate ways.

What is Management?

Management can be an individual or a Company. Either way, they are there to guide the professional career of an Artist, Band or DJ (the **client**) through the highs and lows of the Music Industry. Management may also counsel and advise their client. They should deal with Record Labels, Publishing Houses, Event Organisers and (if they are not qualified) liaise with Solicitors on behalf of their client.

Usually a Management Company will have many Artists/Bands on their books and tend to assign one of their Agents to manage one or often several clients. Some sole Managers may also have more than one client. However, if they are a **one man band** (**stand-alone**) and function without any support, it is often the case that an Artist/Band may feel they are not being represented fully, especially if the Manager has taken on too many clients.

A stand-alone Manager may have to balance many plates. Depending upon how many clients they represent, a stand-alone Manager can be more involved than some Management Companies.

If an Artist/Band is unsigned and unknown, provided it has been agreed, their Management would arrange its client's career path. They would build profile, suggest styling or involve a stylist or style agency to help with image. This could include photo shoots, arranging collaborations between Songwriters and Producers and liaison with Record Labels and Promoters.

What is a Management Contract?

A Management Contract is a legally binding Agreement that an Artist, Band or DJ would sign with either a Manager or Management Company.

A Management Contract is as complex as any other Agreement. Depending on the Code of Practice of the Manager or Management Company, the Contract may contain legally binding restrictions and stipulations as to the Contracting Parties conduct, handling and expected prospects.

The **term** of a Management Contract can be from **one** (1) year to **in perpetuity** (forever). Usually a Management Contract will be for at least 3 to 5 years so that an Artist/Band can be developed. A Management Contract may also contain provisions whereby on termination (by either Party), Management are further entitled to a percentage of an Artist's/Band's earnings. This may be on the same percentage or on a reducing scale over time. The term of this provision can be up to ten years after termination of the Contract. Therefore, (as with all agreements) it is essential to have a Solicitor look over it for you, to ensure that you understand and to make you aware of the details contained within it.

A word of caution, Management may add Clauses into their Contracts or ask you to sign a new Contract whereby your publishing or other rights are assigned to them. There is no good reason for a Songwriter to assign publishing rights over to their Management, unless their Management has a legitimate Publishing Company and they intend to collect and pay out publishing royalties to their client. Even then, it is always best to shop around for the best deal.

Management in today's market

Many moons ago, Management were an integral link in the chain that is the Music Industry. An Artist/Band without Management Representation may not have been taken as seriously as an Artist/Band that was represented.

Times and attitudes have changed and with the growth of the internet, so has evolved a prodigious stage, available to anyone and everyone. The internet is a platform where Artists/Bands can show off their flair and ability whilst attracting fans and media attention without any Management involvement and in some cases without even leaving their bedroom.

The downside however is that the market is crammed with hopefuls and would-be's, making it increasingly difficult for Artists and Bands to stand out.

While an Artist/Band no longer needs Management Representation, there is no doubt that having a third party advocating on their behalf, promoting, supporting, developing career paths and creating opportunities defines one Artist/Band from another. That is, provided said Management keeps up with the ever changing aspects of the Music Industry including promoting and maintaining interest in their client.

Acceptable Management Involvement

Management may assist their clients in arranging collaborations. Developing and building upon already formulated associations within the Music Industry will advance their client's career.

Management may also attend recording sessions, acting as liaison, to support their client and rectify any issues that may occur. Management should carry out this support without any creative intervention, unless this has been previously agreed by their client.

On that basis, it is not reasonable for Management to claim co-writing or a publishing credit, unless there has been *bona fide* input by Management which was agreed in advance by their client.

Subsequent and/or additional fees outside any Management Contract should be negotiated as if it were a new contract. Legal advice should be sought before an Artist/Band signs or agrees in principal to the conditions the Management requests.

Where Management makes all the difference

There have been times where Management really has made all the difference to an Artist/Band. Some Artists/Bands have hopped from Manager to Management Company while they worked their way up the industry ladder.

There is no doubt that Management has to be robust and resilient. Management are forever in the firing line, facing opposition from all sides. Their job can be the hardest in the world. Especially if interest in their client is dwindling or if their client decides to go **off on a tangent** against all that is current, popular or acceptable and more importantly what has been agreed in their Management Contract.

One such success story is that of **Stefani Joanne Angelina Germanotta (Lady Gaga). Troy Carter** of **Coalition Media** signed **Lady Gaga** with the intention of making her into a star. In a paper by **Martin Kupp, Jamie Anderson** and **Joerg Reckhenrich**, they highlighted the approach **Carter, Coalition**

Media and **Lady Gaga** had taken, in their use of the **Four E's** (**emotions**, **experience**, **engagement**, and **exclusivity**). They illustrated **Carter's** online marketing strategy, whereby **Carter**, became aware of the decrease in the Music Industry's total revenue and realised this decline was due to digitalisation. **Carter** acted upon it and with the aid of a marketing company, **ThinkTank Digital**, **Carter** developed **Lady Gaga's** profile through social media. The plan included blogs, exclusive interviews and special features on **Myspace**. Meanwhile **Lady Gaga** managed her own tweets through Twitter, enabling her to connect on a more personal level with her fans through online activity. In quite a short amount of time, **Carter** had managed to move his client from obscurity into a household name and thereby **Lady Gaga** attained superstardom.

Reasons to get involved

One of the advantages of an Artist/Band having Management may be that they can pass over the tedious jobs, leaving the Artist/Band to get on with making music. But if that Artist/Band has no experience of the Music Industry and how it operates, the chances are they may never know, without some kind of involvement on their part.

From a financial standpoint, if an Artist's/Band's Management takes care of every area of business, including royalty payments, Management will undoubtedly take their percentage before the Artist/Band earns anything. Whether out of inexperience or lethargy, when an Artist/Band gives Management *carte blanche* to settle accounts directly from the Artist's/Band's royalty distributions it is difficult to keep track of spending. Also, an Artist/Band will have no idea of how much they have earned or should be earning, how to balance their books or who to deal with should the relationship break down.

So before entering into any legal arrangement with Management, it is worth investigating their historical background. Firstly, check that they are who they say they are. Secondly, ensure that they can back up (with past work references) any important questions you have so you can **rule out** dubious setbacks in areas essential to your career. For instance, if you decided to employ the services of a builder, you would ask to see references and testimonials of past work.

Your prospective Management should be able to explain the fundamental essence of a Contract to you. Prior to signing a Management Contract, it would be prudent to ask any niggling questions, including what is the protocol taken by Management for future Contracts you may be asked to sign.

Most importantly, do not assume that your Manager has a Degree in entertainment law or that your Management Company has the resources to employ a Solicitor who specialises in entertainment law. Find out first-hand how they intend to deal with future contracts on your behalf.

Contracts

Oh what a tangled web we weave, when first we practice to deceive. (Sir Walter Scott -Marmion)

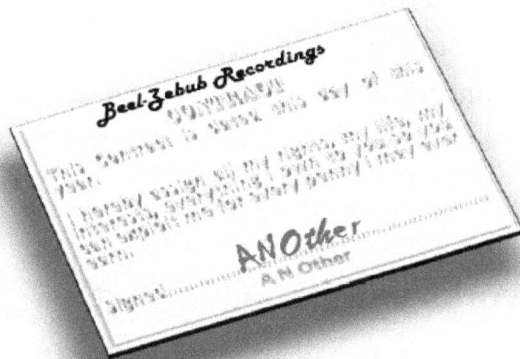

Before you sign your life away, there are some important factors to take into consideration.

What is a Contract?

A written Contract is a legal and binding agreement. If you sign it, you are legally bound by its terms. But bear in mind, legally binding contracts can be made orally by simple principles of offer and acceptance.

However, please note that the law varies from territory to territory, meaning, if you sign a Contract and that Contract is governed by Italian Law, you would need to find an Italian Lawyer to represent you in an Italian Court of Law should the other party prove to be in breach of the Contract.

Also the law evolves and is updated over time. It may be that an area of the law may have been amended, modified or overturned so it is always good to have a Contract looked over by a Solicitor before you commit to sign it.

Bear in mind that if you agree to something in writing via an email, this can also constitute as a binding agreement. It is something I do when I collaborate initially with a co-writer. I state in writing the percentages and terms on which I agree to write the song with them. If they then send me a return email agreeing to my terms, effectively they have entered into a binding agreement and consent to the terms I have set out. This has come in very handy on several occasions when a co-writer has gone back on the splits we originally agreed.

If you are signing a Record Label Contract then it is always best to get the advice of a Solicitor with specialised knowledge of entertainment law.

Many contracts are often written in a complex way, so if you are unsure and do not understand anything do not sign it. In this case, it is best to ask your contact at the Record Label to explain something you are unclear about. If they cannot or are unwilling to explain it then it would be unwise to enter into an agreement with them.

How the Law works within a Contract

In English Law, many contracts will have definitions. These definitions are normally contained within a **Definitions** clause. This is typically an alphabetical list of words used throughout the contract. Each word defined is usually followed by its meaning (as below). Most Record Label contracts tend to contain definitions and terms however many Recording Contracts may not include a definitions clause, so below I have listed some of the common terms used and their meaning:

Advance

A nominated fee given in advance of any future sales your song(s) may make. An advance fee is usually paid back out of mechanical royalties (see **Chapter 11, Royalties**) before an Artist/Band receives any further payment.

Deductions

This means whether the Record Label is allowed to deduct the distribution and/or manufacturing fees from your royalty distribution. For example, if a Record Label has arranged for a Video to be made for your track, then this expenditure would usually be deducted from your royalties before you receive any payment.

Exclusivity

A Recording Contract may include an **Exclusivity clause** which will require an Artist/Band to sign to the Record Label exclusively. This effectively will mean that the Artist/Band cannot work with another Record Label without first getting permission from their Record Label, unless the Artist/Band insists on a **sideman provision** being inserted. Another method of avoiding total exclusivity would be for an Artist/Band to use an **alias** (a different stage name). In having a clause written that any performance or recording undertaken by the Artist/Band as anyone other than the signed alias shall be permitted.

An Exclusivity provision may also mean that an Artist/Band cannot leave the Contract if they are unhappy. However, they can of course terminate the Contract if the Record Label is found to be in breach of the Recording Contract or *vice versa*.

The reason many Record Labels insist on an **Exclusivity clause** is because (especially in the case of a Major Record Label) they invest a lot of money to develop and break a new Artist/Band. In order to recoup their costs and make a profit they deem this a perfunctory part of their Contract.

Ironically, the Record Label is free to sign and promote as many or as few Acts as it feels is appropriate or manageable.

Governing Law

Every Contract is governed by the law of a Territory. Most Record Labels will use the law of their country (i.e. Armada will use Dutch law to govern its contract). Please note: if at any time you had to instruct a Solicitor/Lawyer about a legal issue with a Record Label, you would probably have to have your Solicitor instruct a legal specialist in that Territory.

Rights

Exclusive Rights: Under an **exclusive rights** term, the Record Label owns the exclusive rights to sell the track and decide what to do with it.

Inclusive Rights: Under **inclusive rights** the Artist/Band has more control over the track and can offer it to other Record Labels. It is very **rare** that a Record Label would offer to sign your track inclusively.

Royalty Rate

This is the percentage that indicates how much an Artist/Band will receive from the money their track generates. There will normally be a different percentage for digital, physical and third party releases.

Royalty Statements

Royalty Statements are usually sent out twice a year. The due date for delivery of Statements should be set out in the Contract. It may be up to the Artist/Band to invoice the Record Label. Always check this point with your Record Label if you are unclear about it.

Term

This is the length of time (years) an Artist/Band is bound by the Contract. It can be a **fixed term**, whereby a set time is put in place or it may be **terminable upon notice**. **Terminable upon notice** means that it is a **rolling** Contract and will only be terminated if one party serves notice to the other party or, if both Parties are in agreement that the relationship should come to an end. An Artist/Band may be asked to sign a Contract **in perpetuity**. The meaning of **in perpetuity** is **forever**. If an Artist/Band signs a Contract **in perpetuity**, then they will be unable to renegotiate at a later stage and will lose some of their rights, depending on what other provisions they have signed within the Contract.

Termination

Any Recording Contract should include a clause offering both parties the right to terminate should either of them be in breach of contract. One reason an Artist/Band may feel they want to terminate is if the Record Label should go into liquidation. Equally safeguards should be put in place for both parties for failure to abide by the terms set out in the Contract.

If the Record Label does go into liquidation, the Artist/Band should not only be able to terminate the Contract but they should also have the rights in the recordings revert back to them. Failure to incorporate this provision may mean that the copyright of the recording may then become the property of third-party creditors.

Territory

Territory means the country of origin for the Contract. This is usually where the Record Label is based. Most Recording Contracts sign an Artist/Band for a worldwide deal.

Kinds of Contract

Over time you may come across different kinds of Contract. Listed below are several types of Contract that you may be asked to sign and some of the provisions you should be aware of:

Management Contract

A Management Contract is an arrangement whereby an individual or company has operational control over an Artist's/Band's musical career, in return for a percentage fee.

Recently, some Artists/Bands have been asked by their Management to sign a Production Contract rather than a Management Contract. There is no benefit for an Artist/Band to sign this type of Contract unless their Management have a genuine Production Company. Ultimately, the real benefit in Management insisting on their Artist/Band signing a Production Contract, is that Management then has complete control over the Artist/Band.

Things to look out for are:

Career expectation: is what is expected of both/all Parties. For the Artist/Band this may mean Management promoting them to Record Labels, arranging gigs and taking care of all business.

Fee: is the percentage (between 10%-30%) of earnings that an Artist/Band has agreed to pay to Management in exchange for their services.

Like any Contract, a Management Contract may be over-complicated so it is imperative for an Artist/Band to seek legal advice to ensure their interests are protected.

Good faith: implies that both parties will act honestly, fairly and in good faith.

Mutual benefit: means that the Contract reflects the realistic expectations of both Parties, that they will both derive benefit from the Contract.

Term: you do not want to sign a lifelong agreement so if you cannot find the term, always check with the other Party.

Songwriting Contract

This should be a simple Contract that sets out the writing splits between co-writers.

The copyright within the composition of a co-written song once recorded belongs by an agreed percentage to the co-writers. A Songwriting Contract legalises the co-writers by name, against their share of the composition.

There is no need for a Songwriting Contract to be overly elaborate and I believe the MU may have a specimen of a Songwriting Contract which barely fills half a page.

Collaboration Contract

This Contract is much the same as a Songwriting Contract except it should be in-depth; detailing the provisions the co-writers expect to be bound by.

Things to look out for:

Credit: this refers to the Master and Composition Credits i.e. who performed and wrote the composition.

Duty: some Contracts may put provisions in place that expect certain duties to be carried out by both or one Party (i.e. to keep in contact and for all mailing addresses kept up-to-date).

Fee: some Singer/Songwriters may charge a fee for their Vocal Recording. If a fee is charged, there should be a provision within the Contract setting out the terms of the fee (i.e. whether it is an advance on future royalty).

Good faith: means that all parties will act honestly and fairly with one another.

Governing Law: this will set out the country (territory) of where the Contract will be governed.

Ownership: this provision sets out the percentage of ownership between the co-writers.

Because a Collaboration Contract is between Songwriters it should be self-explanatory but if it seems convoluted in any way, it is always beneficial to get advice.

Publishing: if a Songwriter was published and had already signed a Publishing Contract, then this provision would be put in place to cover this aspect and to clarify that the Songwriter's publishing is already being collected.

Term: this can be anything from 3 years to a rolling term. If the Contract has a rolling term, once the composition is signed to a Record Label, the term within the Recording Contract would dictate the length of your Collaboration Contract. Usually once a composition has been recorded (i.e. the music, vocals and lyrics fused into one composition), the copyright would be jointly owned by co-writers on that particular recording for life.

Use: in terms of the music, vocal and lyric, this provision is put in place so that there is no infringement on the intellectual property of either party.

Intellectual Property Contract

If as a Singer/Songwriter you find you are sending out music or vocals/lyrics and feel unprotected, then an Intellectual Property Contract will safeguard your work. This can be a simple two line Contract, setting out in writing that your work is solely for use on a composition. Stipulate that you do not agree or intend your work to be used on another composition, or used by anyone else, copied, cut up or used in any other way. You can incorporate the provisions of this Contract into a Collaboration Contract.

Recording Contract

The most common type of Recording Contract is where an Artist/Band is signed to a Record Label exclusively. In signing an Exclusive Recording Contract, the Artist/Band will benefit from significant financial and resource investment from the Record Label, for an agreed term for anything from one, three or more albums and for any length of term.

Things to look out for:

Career expectation: is what is expected of both/all Parties. For both Parties, this may mean the release of a certain amount of singles a year or a certain amount of albums produced and released within an agreed period of time.

Good faith: implies that both parties will act honestly and fairly with one another.

Publishing: some Recording Contracts may have a clause in place that includes an Artist's/Band's publishing royalty so it is important to watch for this.

Rate: is the royalty percentage rate that an Artist/Band will receive from the mechanical royalties (see **Chapter 11, Royalties**) achieved by a Record Label.

Term: the term of some Recording Contracts can be lengthy. A Record Label may insist upon a lengthy term because they have to spend money and time in developing an Artist/Band. The term of some Contracts may be **in perpetuity**, which can be extremely difficult to terminate once signed, unless either Party can prove that the other Party is in breach of contract.

Development Contract

In signing a **Development Contract**, an Artist/Band may not have the full support of a Record Label. The provisions contained in this kind of Contract usually set out that the Record Label does not have to commit to the Artist/Band and therefore the risk (predominantly financial loss) to the Record Label is kept at a minimum.

Typically, any Artist/Band signing this type of Contract will be required to record a few singles, so that the Record Label can **test the water** before fully committing and entering into a Recording Contract, based upon the results of these initial recordings.

Things to look out for:

Career expectation: an Artist may not be offered a Recording Contract at the end of a Development Contract.

Publishing: always watch out for any clause that mentions publishing royalty. An Artist/Band may sign away publishing without attaining a Recording Contract.

Rate: is the royalty percentage rate that an Artist/Band will receive from the mechanical royalties (see **Chapter 11, Royalties**) achieved by a Record Label.

Term: the term of the Development Contract. An Artist/Band would not particularly want to sign a lengthy Development Contract, unless there was provision set in place by the Record Label to ensure a Recording Contract would be offered after a set time had elapsed. However, if during the term of the Contract, another Record Label offered to sign the Artist/Band with a full Recording Contract, including the usual benefits, the original Record Company may expect financial recompense from the second Record Label which may impinge on the Artist's/Band's royalty unless agreed otherwise.

Production Contract

A Production Contract is a Contract between an Artist/Band and a Production Company. When signing a Production Contract, the Artist/Band ultimately agrees for the Production Company to act as mediator. The Production Company is then legally able to license the Artist/Band's recordings to a Record Label.

Whilst a Production Company may persuade an Artist/Band that in signing their Production Contract it may quantify as a step towards global recognition, it is worth noting that it is very rare for an Artist/Band to then go on and sign with a Major Record Label.

Things to look out for:

Career expectation: is what is expected of both/all Parties. The Artist/Band may have to produce a required amount of songs. The Production Company may be expected to licence a required amount of songs. If this provision is in place, this should be clarified as to the financial benefit to the Artist/Band in any license attained.

Good faith: implies that both parties will act honestly, fairly and in good faith.

Percentage: the percentage amount of an Artist/Band's earnings they have contractually agreed to pay to the Production Company for its services.

Rights: the Artist/Band may have to sign away some or all rights. Also there may be options contained within the Contract enforcing a long term commitment.

Term: the term of some Production Contracts can be **in perpetuity** and if a Record Label offers to sign an Artist/Band this may be extremely difficult to terminate without proof of breach of contract or the Production Company expecting a big pay-off from a Record Label.

360 Contract

Where a Recording Contract allows a Record Label to profit from an Artist/Band by selling their recordings, a **360 Contract** allows a Record Label to profit from all financially viable aspects attached to the Artist/Band (i.e. merchandise, tours, etc.)

Care should be taken by an Artist/Band Member when signing a 360 Contract if the Artist/Band Member also has a career in say, acting or is a writer, as there may be provision within this type of Contract for a Record Label to claim financial benefit from this alternative work.

I have been asked by Management to sign a similar provision which would have bound me into a Contract that would have meant my Manager took a percentage of any other fiscal gain made from creative sources. Again I can only reiterate that as with **ALL** contracts do get it checked over and watch out for these pitfalls.

Things to look out for:

Career expectation: is what is expected of both/all Parties. The Record Label may expect a fee from the Artist/Band Member for financial activity outside of Songwriting.

Good faith: implies that both parties will act honestly, fairly and in good faith.

Percentage: the percentage amount from an Artist/Band Member's earnings they have contractually agreed to pay to the Record

Company when the Artist/Band Member receives money from another source.

Rights: there may be provisions contained within the Contract allowing the Record Label to enforce a long term commitment, so that the Record Label continues to benefit financially on future earnings of the Artist/Band Member outside of Songwriting.

Term: the term of any Contract should be noted and discussed. Always watch out for the words **in perpetuity** in any Contract.

Performance / Touring Contract

If you sign to a Major Record Label you may be asked to sign a Performance / Touring Contract. This encompasses much of the above clauses within the 360 Contract, in that a Record Label benefits and profits in a **Captain Kirk win-win scenario**. The Artist/Band goes on the road, the ticket sales pay for the cost of the tour and a percentage of the profit will go to the Record Label before the Artist/Band earns a bean.

Things to look out for:

Career expectation: is what is expected of both/all Parties. The Record Label may expect the Artist/Band to tour on a regular basis.

Good faith: implies that both parties will act honestly, fairly and in good faith.

Rate/Percentage: is the amount an Artist/Band may receive, depending on the cost of the tour. Watch out for sundries and unexplainable costs.

Term: the term of any Contract should be noted and discussed. Always watch out for the words **in perpetuity** in any Contract.

Publishing Contract

A Publishing Contract is a Contract set out between a Songwriter and a Publishing Company. It is a Contract that assigns to a Publishing Company, the right to collect royalties on behalf of a Songwriter's work for an agreed percentage fee. There is usually a minimum term of three years. This is based on the time it may take for a Publisher to collate the information for royalties to be collected, as this can take some time, especially when the Songwriter is prolific.

The usual and fair percentage rate up to now has been 20%. However, it has been heard recently for a Publishing Company to take 50% of a Songwriter's publishing royalty. If a Songwriter has signed a Publishing Contract with a well-known Publisher, who guarantees synchronisations and licensing thus creating more income for the Songwriter, then this high percentage may be a slightly less bitter pill to swallow.

Things to look out for:

Career expectation: is what is expected of both/all Parties. The Artist/Band may have to contract to the Publishing Company a required amount of songs or sign over the whole catalogue of their work.

Good faith: implies that both parties will act honestly, fairly and in good faith.

Rate: is the royalty percentage rate that an Artist/Band will receive from the Publishing royalties (see **Chapter 11, Royalties**) after the Publishing Company has taken their agreed percentage. This rate seems to be increasing in favour of the Publishing Company, so it is always a good idea to enter into negotiations before you sign a Publishing Contract, thus ensuring you get the best deal.

Rights: the Artist/Band may have to sign away some or all rights.

Term: the term of some Publishing Contracts can be lengthy so you need to watch out for the term, especially the words **in perpetuity**.

If you are asked to sign a Contract, remember to take your time to review it or preferably get legal advice. Before signing any document, it is important that you are happy with all the provisions contained within it.

Publishing

And you must cut this flesh from off his breast. The law allows it, and the court awards it. (William Shakespeare – The Merchant of Venice)

When you write and perform on a track, this will be known as a composition. Publishing relates to the copyright of a composition and if you have written this work alone, the copyright of the work is owned by you 100%.

If you have co-written the song with another Songwriter, the composition will belong to both of you, usually on an equal basis depending on what you have agreed to prior to commencement of the work.

If your work has been released, sold and played then you may be able to collect publishing royalty, dependent upon the exposure your song has received.

A Publisher is usually a company who can collect and administer all the streams of revenues. If you have signed a Publishing Contract with a Publisher, this will mean that you have assigned the copyright of your composition to that Publishing Company and they will collect your royalties and pay it to you bi-annually.

If you do not have a Publishing Contract with a Publishing Company then your work will be categorised as **copyright control**. This means that you are the self-collecting and self-administrating percentage owner of any financial royalty attached to that composition, once it has been used commercially. In the UK, you can collect independently through **PRS** for Music. (See **Chapter 15, Collection Societies**.)

Where does a Publisher collect from?

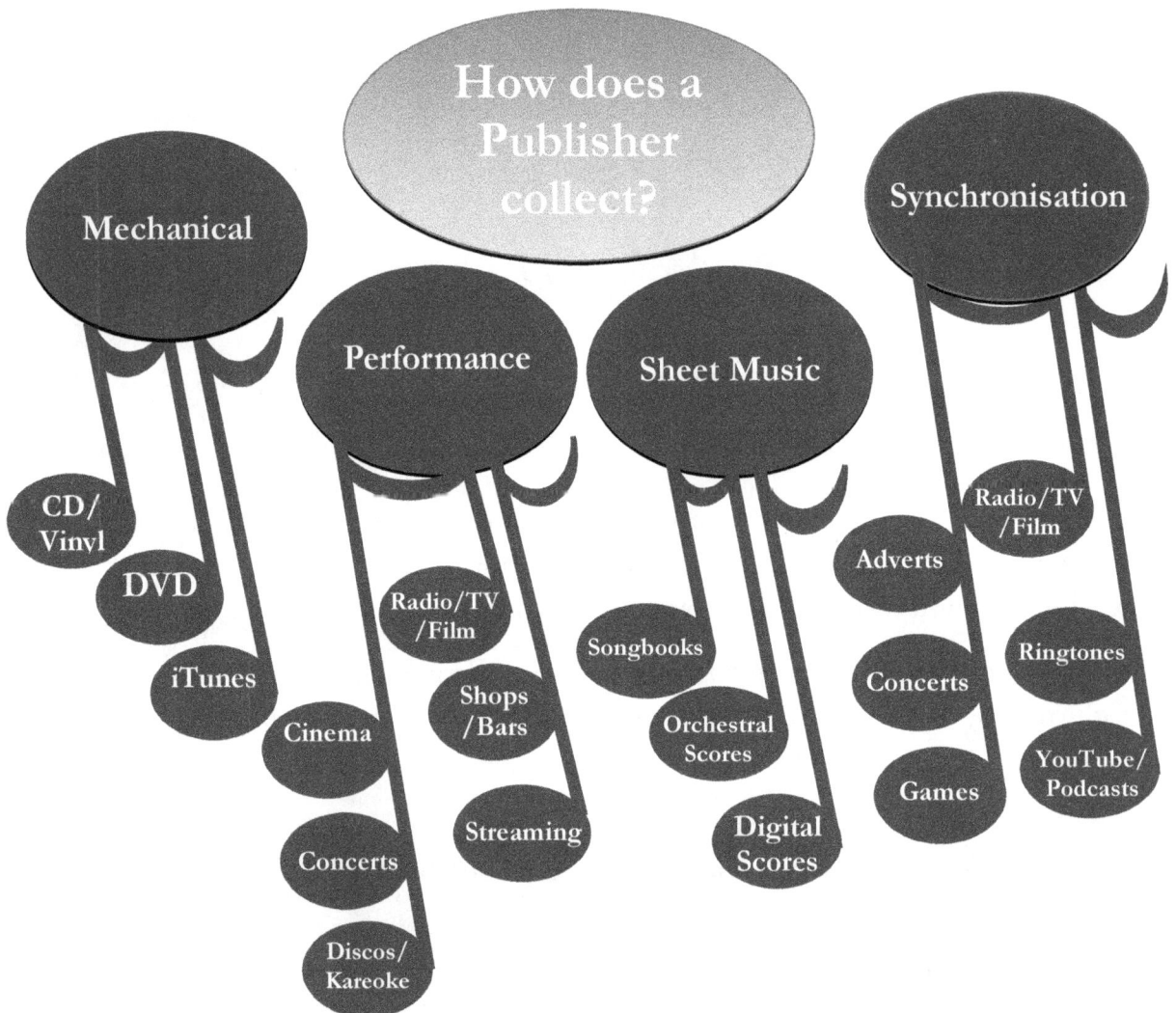

How does a Publisher collect?

Mechanical
- CD/Vinyl
- DVD
- iTunes

Performance
- Radio/TV/Film
- Cinema
- Shops/Bars
- Concerts
- Streaming
- Discos/Kareoke

Sheet Music
- Songbooks
- Orchestral Scores
- Digital Scores

Synchronisation
- Radio/TV/Film
- Adverts
- Concerts
- Ringtones
- Games
- YouTube/Podcasts

Sheet Music:	Mechanical:	Performance:	Synchronisation:
Songbooks	CD / Vinyl	Radio	Advertising
Scores for orchestras	LPs/Singles	Television / Cable	Films
Digital scores	DVDs	Streaming services	Television shows
	iTunes / Amazon etc.	Shops/Bars	Radio production
		Discotheques	Video games
		Cinemas	Podcasts
		Karaokes	YouTube videos
		Concerts	Ringtones
		Any public event where music is played	

If you decide to sign a Publishing Contract, the Publishing Company may offer you an advance (a lump sum). Let us say in this instance you have been given £20k in advance fees. Unless you have a provision set in place within your Publishing Contract stating otherwise, you will not earn any royalty from your Publishing Company until this advance fee has been paid back.

Often a Publishing Company may use the services of another Publishing Company, in order to exploit their catalogue. This is defined as Sub-Publishing and a separate Sub-Publishing Contract would be put in place between your Publishing Company and the new Sub-Publisher.

It is worth bearing in mind that some Recording Contracts often insert a publishing clause in their Contracts just for good measure, so it is vital to always read the fine print. Otherwise you may sign your publishing away by accident. This could cause you untold problems if you have already signed your publishing over to a Publishing Company.

Royalties

"When I was young I thought that money was the most important thing in life; now that I am old I know that it is." Oscar Wilde

S o you have released your first track. The next and most important thing to do is make sure you are registered with the **Collection Societies**. (See **Chapter 15, Collection Societies**.) If not, you cannot collect any royalty distributions and therefore you will not receive any money.

With the development of the internet and technology, it is now easier for these companies to collect on your behalf. But it is still complex and every now and then a track may slip through the net, so it is imperative to keep abreast of your tracks or have someone to help you do this.

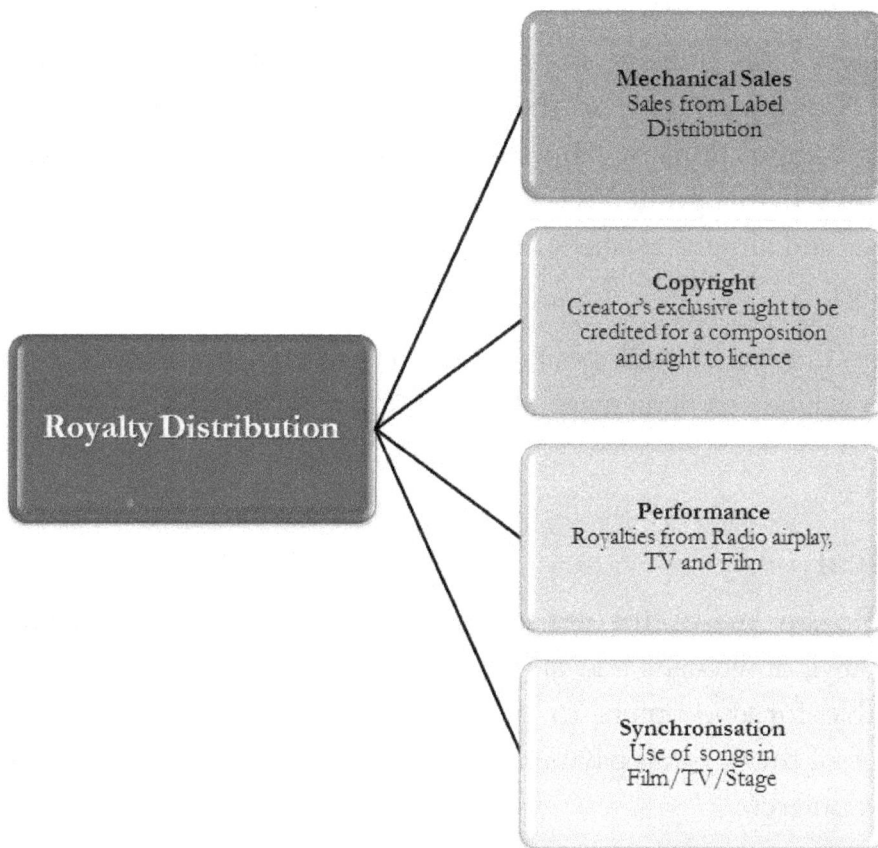

What are royalties?

There are four types of royalty:

Sheet Music:	Mechanical:	Performance:	Synchronisation:
Songbooks	CD / Vinyl LPs/Singles	Radio	Advertising
Scores for orchestras	DVDs	Television / Cable	Films
Digital scores	iTunes / Amazon etc.	Streaming services	Television shows
		Shops/Bars	Radio production
		Discotheques	Video games
		Cinemas	Podcasts
		Karaokes	YouTube videos
		Concerts	Ringtones
		Any public event where music is played	

Sheet Music

When a piece of music is created, that composition belongs to the Songwriter(s)/Composer(s). In the past, Composers would write their musical notations and compositions by hand and this was entitled **sheet music**. Today, sheet music usually refers to a printed score which is then sold at a fee. Often Artists/Bands sell their songs and albums as sheet music in book form, so that their fans can learn to play their songs.

A Songwriter/Composer will be entitled to revenue from sales of sheet music, however, this will be at a percentage after printing and other costs have been deducted.

Mechanical

Mechanical Royalty means the per-unit payments for the reproduction of work on CDs, MP3, vinyl, downloads and all other formats that a Record Label produces and makes available for consumers to purchase. A Songwriter will receive an agreed percentage fee of the per-unit payment, which is defined by a mechanical licence within a Recording Contract.

If another Artist/Band recorded their version of a Songwriter's song, they would need a mechanical licence in order to be able to legally release their version.

Performance

Performance Royalty is a royalty paid to the performer of the song. This is collected by the Performance Rights Organisations like PPL, ASCAP, SoundExchange etc. In order to claim from this royalty, you would need to be a member of one of these organisations.

Users of music in a public place, say a hairdressers, must buy a licence to be able to play music in their hair salon. They should then fill out a form, stating what music they have played, enabling each Songwriter to receive their entitled share of the Performance Royalty.

To determine what music has been performed and which members should receive payment for their performances, production companies are responsible for sending **cue sheets** to the organisation of their respective territory (i.e. PPL in the United Kingdom). These cue sheets list all the music used in any particular program, which once received by the Performance Right Organisation are then tallied to broadcast schedules and performances and processed so that Songwriters receive royalties. However, there is often a limited time for a Songwriter to claim this royalty, so it is beneficial to know which song(s) and its date of use, so you can inform your Collection Agency.

A bone of contention for many Songwriters is the Live Performances/Public Use at concerts, festivals and organised club nights. This is because Collection Agencies rely upon DJs/Festival Organisers and Promoters to fill out forms, confirming their set lists, thus ensuring that a Songwriter receives a royalty for the use of their song. If a DJ/Festival Organiser and/or a Promoter fails to carry out this important task the Songwriter loses out.

Synchronisation

Synchronisation royalty is created each time a Songwriter's composition is used within a film, TV show, advertisement, stage performance etc. Prior permission in the form of a licence has to be given to a person, company or entity involved in the theatre, film, or TV industry wishing to incorporate a Songwriter's composition into their production. The royalty percentage attained by the Songwriter would be agreed prior to the use of the composition, either by the Songwriter, the Songwriter's Publisher or Record Label, depending on where the vested authority lay to agree to the licence.

Back Catalogues and Licensing

"Being good in business is the most fascinating kind of art. Making money is art and working is art and good business is the best art." (Andy Warhol)

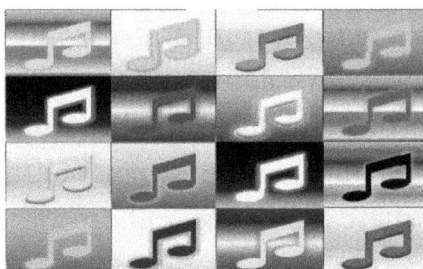

It seems Record Labels must have their fingers in many pies in order to keep the cash rolling in. Whilst much negotiation goes on behind the scenes, possibly the easiest earner is the Licensing and Back Catalogue sales. These sales are received by a Record Label when they sell their signed Artist's/Band's work onto other Companies for onward distribution. This can be in various areas and territories, selling songs onto distributors or selling licenses to songs in the many entertainment mediums available to them.

Licensing

As mentioned in the Royalty section, in the UK, the use of recorded music in public, usually, legally requires a licence from PPL on behalf of the performer and from PRS on behalf of the Songwriter /Composer or their Publisher.

Music Licensing is the legal use, through a licence, for the buying and selling of music, music that has been pre-negotiated for a fee for its distribution.

If you are an Artist/Band signed to a Record Label, your Record Label may sell your work to another Record Label for distribution in another territory or for use on a compilation CD. For an established Artist/Band this could be a **best of album**. This is a further source of revenue for the Record Label, as they will negotiate and receive a fee for this licence.

Again, this is something you should check before signing your Recording Contract, as to whether there is provision in place that will entitle you to a percentage of the fee that your Record Label receives for such licensing.

Happy Birthday to You is an exaggerated example of how licensing can work effectively. The song was originally written by **Mildred** and **Patty Hill** in 1893 (although their original words were changed). Warner/Chappell shrewdly bought the rights to the song, allowing them a hefty profit every year in millions of pounds worth of licensing fees.

Happy Birthday is a Guinness World Record Holder and to date the most profitable song ever.

Back Catalogues

A lucrative arrangement for Record Labels (especially the Major Record Labels who have a wealth of Artists/Bands in their arsenal), is the sale and resale of the back catalogues of their established Artists/Bands.

The cost of establishing new Artists and Bands offers no financial safeguard for these magnates. Having a dependable and profitable return on recognised **iconic** and **classic** albums, helps to entice the music buying public into purchasing **must have** and **collector** albums, as well as **Anniversary Box Sets**.

Just recently there has been an up-turn in a younger audience buying records, a new generation of music consumers. These new consumers are eager to experience the feel and sound of vinyl and to discover Artists/Bands and influences from the yester eras.

Despite the internet making it much easier for Record Labels and Distributors to sell their wares, the Major Record Labels are regularly contesting with each other, bidding for the rights to buy the high profile back catalogues of **The Beatles, The Rolling Stones, Frank Sinatra** amongst others.

It was rumoured that one of the Major Record Labels, who already owned half of **The Rolling Stones** catalogue recently paid £10 million to buy the remaining half from another Record Label, alongside signing a new recording deal with the band.

Copyright Protection

Composers and Songwriters should know how to protect their work.

Copyright is a legal concept that gives the creator of an original work (this includes literary, dramatic, musical, graphic and audio-visual creations) exclusive rights to it. Generally, this means the **right to copy** or **reproduce the work**. However, it also gives the copyright holder the right to be credited for the work, prohibits adaption of the work into other forms or its public performance and so in effect, who may financially benefit from the work.

According to UK Law, the Copyright, Designs and Patents Act 1988 (last amended 2003) (**CDPA**) advises that once you have recorded your work it is protected automatically by copyright law, so that there is no requirement to register a work to obtain copyright protection.

In 1887 the UK signed the Berne Convention. The Berne Convention recognised that the copyright for a creative work does not have to be claimed, instead the copyright is automatically set in place at creation ergo a Composer need not register their claim for copyright. Thus a copyright holder's authenticity of all copyrights in the work is confirmed in the countries who have signed the Berne Convention until the expiry of copyright.

How do you protect your music as a Songwriter?

In the UK, all original music is protected by copyright from the time it is recorded/written down in some format. But it is important to be able to prove that you own the copyright of a particular recording.

One way of doing this is to send a copy of the recording to yourself by post. Mark the envelope so you know what work is contained inside but **do not** open it. It **must** remain sealed and with the date of postage on it. You can also store a copy of your work that you wish to copyright with a Solicitor or your Bank Manager. In this event, you will need to keep a note of its existence and it is worth bearing in mind, this latter method is likely to cost money whereas the former will cost you just the price of postage.

A little tip: before you hand out your work to the public it is a good idea to mark any packaging or the CD itself with the copyright holder's name, the copyright symbol © and the year the work was created:

ANOther © 2013

It is not necessarily going to stop an infringement but it certainly shows third parties that it is owned and covered by copyright law and you have some knowledge of what your rights are.

What are your rights as a Copyright Owner?

If you own the copyright you possess the sole authority to:

Copy the music
Issue, lend or rent copies to the public
Perform, show or play the music in public
Communicate the music to the public (i.e. broadcasting it via TV, radio, Internet etc.)

Under UK Law, the duration of copyright is the whole life of the creator plus seventy (70) years from the creator's death.

Copyright for the Singer / Songwriter

There is much confusion within the industry about copyright, in that some still believe that when an author of lyrics / vocal melody writes with a musical Composer the copyright in its entirety of lyrics, vocal melody and music belongs to both parties.

The lyrics of a song are protected as a literary work and the copyright in the lyrics belongs to the writer of the lyrics. This copyright is known as the **Original Literary Work**.

The music of a song is protected as a musical composition and belongs to the Composer of the music. This copyright is known as the **Original Musical Work**.

Both literary and musical copyrights have the same length of protection and, of course, in many cases the writer of the lyrics and the Composer of the music may be one and the same person.

Once any **Original Literary Work** and **Original Musical Work** are merged into a composition and recorded, it is only then they attract a separate, copyright called the **Sound Recording Copyright**. This copyright belongs in the first instance to the production company or the producers of the work. So someone who makes **pirate** copies of a sound recording of a song will infringe three separate copyrights i.e.: (i) the music; (ii) the lyrics; and (iii) the sound recording.

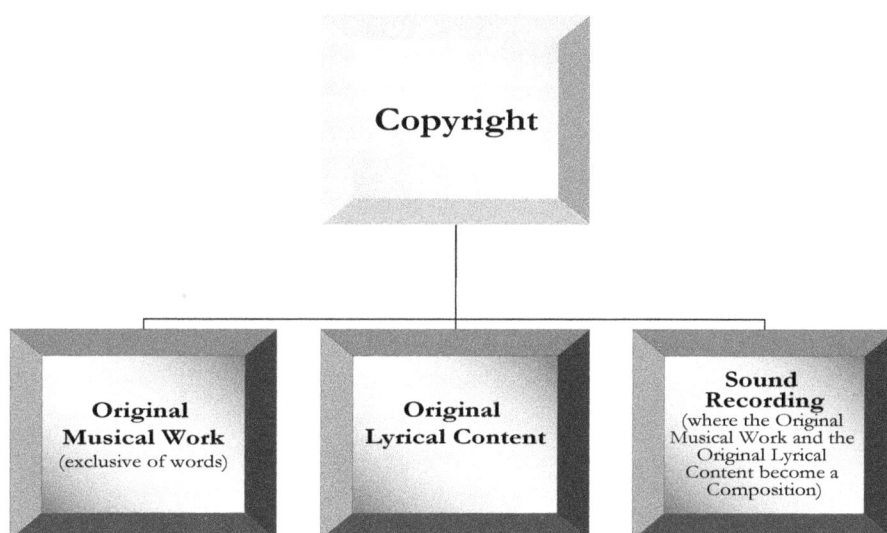

```
                        Copyright
                            |
        +-------------------+-------------------+
        |                   |                   |
    Original            Original            Sound
    Musical Work        Lyrical Content     Recording
    (exclusive of words)                    (where the Original
                                            Musical Work and the
                                            Original Lyrical
                                            Content become a
                                            Composition)
```

Copyright Infringement

Copyright of your composition is one of the most important forms of intellectual property.

Copyright holders generally have full control over their work which gives them the exclusive right to permit or deny a third party the right to copy, perform, show, broadcast, translate, adapt upload, distribute and rent the work to the public. Copyright protection wholly allows the copyright holder complete control in deciding how their work can be used and who can use it.

Copyright is infringed when a copyright holder has not given permission to a third party for any of the above mentioned uses. Copyright infringement occurs regardless whether a third party has used all or part of the work directly or indirectly.

Once a breach of copyright has been discovered or reported, a copyright holder then has the right to take legal action. However, copyright is a private right. Enforcing legal action will depend on the copyright holder's financial or personal circumstances and the extent to which the copyright has been breached.

Intellectual Property

Intellectual Property has nothing to do with buying a house.

Intellectual Property (**IP**) is the generic term used to describe those creations of the human mind which the law protects. In broad terms, Intellectual Property falls into five main categories:

What counts as Intellectual Property?
- Brands or logos
- An invention
- Design (for a product both shape and surface decoration)
- Written content (book, brochure, website)
- Artistic content (Photography, paintings, illustrations)
- Film (video/digital)
- Musical compositions
- Computer software

What is NOT Intellectual Property?

An **idea** of itself is not recognised.

If the idea involves an invention it may be capable of protection as a patent. If it is in the artistic field, then once written down, drawn or otherwise recorded, it will likely be protected as copyright work. Copyright will also protect preliminary works i.e. a synopsis for a book.

Who owns Intellectual Property?

If you create something, you would usually own the intellectual property.

If you are employed or subcontracted to create something or if you employ or sub-contract someone to create something, a Contract should be put in place that clarifies who owns the intellectual property.

Protecting your Intellectual Property Rights?

By putting simple measures in place to protect your intellectual property will afford you rights to prevent a third party from being able to use what you have created without your permission. Similarly it will allow you to charge a third party for the right to use what you have created.

Remember though, responsibility to enforce intellectual property rights lies with their owner. If you feel that your IP rights have been breached and you are unsure of your legal position take the precaution of asking for advice before you start legal proceedings or enter into a dispute.

Getting Protected?

It will depend on what you have created as to what kind of protection you will need:

Copyright

Protects:

> *Literary and written work (books or content on websites)*
> *Dramatic, Performance, Musical, Artistic compositions*
> *TV, Film, Sound and Music recordings*
> *Computer software*
> *Illustrations, Paintings and Photography*

Design Rights

Protects:

> *The physical shape of something original that you design i.e. glassware with a distinctive patterns or style*

Patents

Protects:

> *Inventions that are:*
> *new and not a modification of something else*
> *design that can be physically made*

Trade Marks

Protects:

> *A Logo*
> *A Sound*

Intellectual Property when "pitching"?

Thanks to the internet, it is relatively easy to set up **alerts** on a computer to monitor the use of a Singer/Songwriter's work. Obviously this only works if the user has been open and honest and credited the Singer/Songwriter.

On occasion, you may be affected by or hear about plagiarism of a song, use of a vocal or a sample without permission or no regard for copyright or intellectual property rights.

To pre-empt such events, when sending out work that is not published, say for a pitch or approval by a co-writer, it may be a good idea to use a disclaimer at the bottom or within the text of any messages you send out. This text should state that the work is owned by you, it is your sole and exclusive intellectual property which is covered by copyright. Any breach of use by a third party will amount to action being taken and possible legal proceedings being enforced.

Image and Personality Rights

Under UK law, there is no general right protecting one's image. Instead, those who feel their image or fame have been misappropriated in a commercial context will have to bring a claim for **passing off** or, where appropriate, registered trade mark infringement. Of course, where an unauthorised photograph has been used, the owner of the copyright in the photograph may sue for copyright infringement.

Most Recording Contracts will have a clause inserted that allows the Record Label to use images of their Artists/Bands so that they may promote them and their work. This is yet another contractual issue you will need to watch out for.

Collection Societies

"Fame, I have already. Now I need the money." Wilhelm Steinitz

So you have released your first track. Do not assume that you are automatically going to start reaping the rewards of your hard work. First of all, the most important thing to do is make sure you are registered with the **Collection Societies**. If not, you cannot collect any royalty distributions and therefore you will not receive any money.

Record Labels and Publishers rely on the collection societies such as PRS and MCPS in the UK, to supply them with accurate figures and payment so they can then pay you your percentage of royalty owed.

Promoters are expected to buy a license from PPL and PRS that allows them to legally play music in public. These Promoters, along with DJs and event organisers, are required to submit set lists so that PPL and PRS can allot royalties for the music that has been played.

Unfortunately, sometimes set lists are not handed in. Despite this being one of the main revenues from PPL and PRS, it means few if any Singers/Songwriters will receive a royalty from these types of events and a massive percentage of potential royalties are never distributed.

PPL and PRS for Music are two separate companies. While they both license the use of music and collect royalties for the music industry, they represent different rights holders and have separate licences, terms and conditions.

PPL collects and distributes money for the use of recorded music on behalf of Record Labels and Performers, while PRS for Music collects and distributes money for the use of music and lyrics on behalf of Songwriters, Composers and Publishers.

PRS for Music

 Originally MCPS and PRS were two separate entities. They have since merged and although the legal entities **Mechanical-Copyright Protection Society**, **Performing Right Society** and **MCPS-PRS Alliance** will remain unaffected, the brands will be replaced by **PRS for Music**. **PRS for Music** is accountable to its 95,000-strong members that include rock and pop writers, classical composers, TV and film score composers, library music creators and music publishers.

After deducting the running costs of the organisation, all income received from licence fees is distributed back to its members.

They are the UK's leading Collection Society and part of a global network of Collection Societies. In most cases a licence from PRS for Music will give those who want to use music, the legal right to use copyrighted songs and music compositions registered around the world.

They have around 150 agreements with Collection Societies in nearly 100 countries. These Societies collect and distribute royalties for performances in their country, distribute to their own members, as well as to our members.

Performing Rights Royalties are paid to a Songwriter, Composer or Publisher whenever their music is played or performed in any public space or place. This includes TV, radio, online, in a shop, an office, pub or restaurant, at a concert, a sporting event and thousands of other places.

Eligibility: You are eligible to join the **PRS** if you are:

> *writing your own music*
>
> *your music is being performed at local gigs to national radio*

You can start earning money from your music once you are a member. You do not need to have signed a Contract with a Music Publisher or Record Company.

Mechanical Rights Royalties are paid to the Songwriter, Composer or Publisher when music is reproduced as a physical product or for broadcast or online.

Eligibility: You are eligible to join **MCPS** if you have a piece of music in your catalogue that has been:

> *released commercially by a record company, or*
>
> *recorded into a radio or TV programme, or*
>
> *recorded in an audio-visual or multimedia production, or*
>
> *used online*

Membership and helpful information can be found at: http://www.prsformusic.com

If you have Management, they may register the forms for you but your signature will be required. Be aware that Management may use their own bank details to ensure that this royalty is credited directly to them, thus safeguarding the payment of their percentage fee and gaining them interest before you earn anything.

PPL

In short, PPL is an organisation in the UK that collects royalties for recorded music on behalf of Performers and Rights Holders.

If you have performed on, in any capacity, recorded music or you own the rights to recorded music that may have been broadcast, played in public or on the radio, you could be entitled to royalties.

You are eligible to join PPL if you have performed on recorded music. Becoming a member is free.

However, you will only earn royalties once your tracks have gained airplay and once you make a claim against those tracks.

Due to lack of knowledge there are millions of pounds left unclaimed by Singers and Musicians.

PPL is one of the most pro-active collection agencies in the world and in joining, PPL will help to ensure that you get all the performance royalties that are due to you. If you are not a member you will lose all your royalties if you do not make a claim.

Membership and helpful information can be found at: http://www.ppluk.com.

As with the forms for PRS, if you have Management, they can register on your behalf. If Management enter in their own bank details in the section for royalty distribution instead of yours this royalty will be paid to them directly. Management will pay you after contractual deductions and in their own time.

Worldwide Collection, Copyright and Licensing Organisations

AFRICA		
	KOPIKEN - The Reproduction Rights Society of Kenya	www.kopiken.org/
	MCSK - Music Copyright Society of Kenya	www.mcsk.or.ke/
	KAMP - Kenya Association of Music Producers	www.kamp.or.ke/

ARGENTINA		
	SADAIC - Sociedad Argentina de Autores y Compositores de Musica Argentina Society of Authors and Composers of Music	www.sadaic.org.ar/

AUSTRALIA		
	APRA / AMCOS - Australasian Performing Right Association / Australasian Mechanical Copyright Owners Society	www.apra-amcos.com.au/

AUSTRIA

AKM - Autoren, Komponisten und Musikverleger Authors, Composers and Publishers

www.akm.at/

BELGIUM

SABAM - Société Belge des Auteurs, Compositeurs et Editeurs Belgian Society of Authors, Composers and Publishers

www.sabam.be/

BRAZIL

ECAD - Escritório Central de Arrecadação e Distribuição Central Bureau of Collection and Distribution

www.ecad.org.br/viewco ntroller/publico/Home.a spx

UBC - União Brasileira de Compositores Brazilian Union of Composers

http://www.ubc.org.br/e n/

CANADA

SOCAN

SOCAN - Society of Composers, Authors and Music Publishers of Canada

www.socan.ca/

CHILE

MPLC - Motion Picture Licensing Corporation Chile

www.mplc.cl/

SCD - Sociedad Chilena del Derecho de Autor

www.scd.cl/

COLOMBIA		
	ACINPRO - Society of Authors and Composers SAYCO Colombia and the Colombian Association of Performers and Phonogram Producers	www.saycoacinpro.org.co /quienessomos.php

CROATIA		
	ZAMP - Croatian Composers' Society	www.zamp.hr/home/ho me_en.htm

CYPRUS		
	Asteras - Collective Rights Management	www.asteras.com.cy/

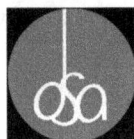

CZECH REPUBLIC		
	OSA - Ochranný svaz autorský pro práva k dílům hudebním (authors of music and lyrics)	www.osa.cz/osa--- english.aspx
	INTERGRAM - music interpreters, audio publishers, audiovisual publishers	www.intergram.cz/en/

DENMARK		
	KODA - Danish and international copyrights for music creators and publishers	www.koda.dk/eng/home /

ESTONIA	
EAU - Estonian Authors' Society	www.eau.org/?lang=eng

FINLAND	
Kopiosto - Copyright organization for authors, publishers and performing artists	www.kopiosto.fi/fi_FI/
Teosto - Authors and Composers of musical works	www.teosto.fi/en
Gramex - performers and publishers of musical works)	www.gramex.fi/en

FRANCE	
SACEM - Société des auteurs, compositeurs et éditeurs de musique Society of Composers, Authors and Music Publishers	www.sacem.fr/cms/site/ en/home?pop=1
SEAM - Société des éditeurs et auteurs de musique Society Publishers and Music Authors	www.seamfrance.fr/

GERMANY	
GEMA - Gesellschaft für musikalische Aufführungs- und mechanische Vervielfältigungsrechte Society for musical performing and mechanical reproduction rights	www.gema.de/en/home. html

GREECE	
AEPI - The Hellenic Society for the Protection of Intellectual Property	www.aepi.gr/index.php?lang=en

HONG KONG	
CASH - Composers and Authors Society of Hong Kong Limited	www.cash.org.hk/en/index.php

HUNGARY	
EJI - Hungarian Performer's Rights	www.eji.hu/english/english.html
Artisjus - Society Artisjus Hungarian Bureau for the Protection Of Authors' Rights	www.artisjus.hu/index_en.php

ICELAND	
STEF - The Performing Rights Society of Iceland	www.stef.is/english

INDIA	
IPRS - (Indian Performing Rights Organization)	www.iprs.org/cms/
PPL - India	www.pplindia.org/

ISRAEL	
	ACUM - representing Authors, Composers, Lyricists, Poets, Arrangers and Music Publishers. www.acum.org.il/english /activity-scope

ITALY	
	SIAE - Società Italiana degli Autori ed Editori Italian Society of Authors and Publishers www.siae.it/index.asp

JAPAN	
JASRAC	JASRAC - Japanese Society for Rights of Authors, Composers and Publishers www.jasrac.or.jp/ejhp/in dex.htm

KOREA (SOUTH)	
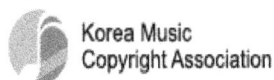	KOMCA - Korea Music Copyright Association www.komca.or.kr/eng/in dex_eng.jsp

LATVIA	
	LaIPA - Latvian Performers and Producers Association www.laipa.org/en
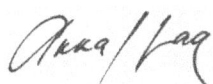	AKKA / LAA - The Latvian authors' society www.akka-laa.lv/eng/

LITHUANIA	
	LATGA www.latga.lt/en

MALAYSIA

	MACP - Music Authors' Copyright Protection	www.macp.com.my/
	PRISM - Performers & Artistes Rights Malaysia	www.prism.org.my/
	PPM - Public Performance Malaysia	www.ppm.org.my/v2/main.asp

MAURITIUS

	MASA - Mauritius Society of Authors	www.gov.mu/portal/sites/ncb/masa/index.html

MEXICO

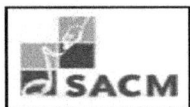

	SACM - General Society of Authors and Composers of Mexico	www.sacm.org.mx/

MIDDLE EAST - ARMENIA

	ARMAUTHOR - Authors' Rights Protection Organization	www.armauthor.am/

NEPAL

	MRCSN - Music Royalty Collection Society Nepal	www.mrcsn.com/

NEW ZEALAND		
	PPNZ - Music Licensing	www.ppnz.co.nz/
	APRA - New Zealand	www.apra.co.nz/

NIGERIA		
	COSON - Copyright Society of Nigeria	www.cosonng.com/

NORWAY		
	TONO - Copyright collective for Authors and Composers of musical works	http://www.tono.no/An dre+sider/English
	GRAMO - Joint Collecting Society in Norway for Musicians, Performing Artists and Phonogram Producers	https://gramo.no/englis h
	NCB - Nordisk Copyright Bureau	www.ncb.dk/

PERU		
	APDAYC - the Peruvian Association of Authors and Composers	www.apdayc.org.pe/

PHILIPPINES

	FILSCAP - Filipino Society of Composers, Authors and Publishers	www.filscap.com.ph/
	PRSP - Performing Rights Society of the Philippines	philmusicregistry.net/main/home

POLAND

ZAiKS	ZAiKS - Union of Writers, Composers and Performers	www.zaiks.org.pl/

PORTUGAL

SPAUTORES	SPA - Portuguese Society of Authors	www.spautores.pt/
gda	GDA - Copyright of Artists and Performers	www.gda.pt/?cat=1

PUERTA RICO

acemla	ACEMLA - Compositors and Publishers Association of Music	www.acemla.com/home/?&lang=en

REPUBLIC OF IRELAND

IMRO	IMRO - Irish Music Rights Organisation	www.imro.ie/
PPI The Music Licensing Company	PPI - Phonographic performance Ireland	www.ppimusic.ie/

ROMANIA		
	UCMR-ADA - Romanian Musical Performing and Mechanical Rights Association	www.ucmr-ada.ro/en/

RUSSIA		
RUSSIAN AUTHORS' SOCIETY	RAO - Russian Authors' Society	www.rao.ru/index.php/en/

SINGAPORE		
	COMPASS - Composers and Authors Society of Singapore	www.compass.org.sg/

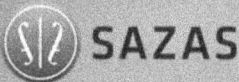

SLOVAKIA		
SAZAS	SAZAS - Association SAZAS	www.sazas.org/domov/english-forms.aspx
SAZOR GIZ	SAZOR GIZ - Slovenian Organization of Authors and Publishers for Reproduction Rights	www.sazor.si/en/

SOUTH AFRICA		
SAMRO	SAMRO - Southern African Music Rights Organisation	www.samro.org.za/
NORM	NORM - National Organisation for Reproduction Rights of Music in South Africa	www.norm.co.za/

SPAIN

| | SGAE - General Society of Authors and Editors | www.sgae.es/ |

SWEDEN

| | STIM - Swedish Performing Right Society | www.stim.se/en/ |

SWITZERLAND

| | SUISA - Cooperative Society of Music Authors and Publishers in Switzerland | www.suisa.ch/en/ |
| | SSA - Swiss Authors Society | www.ssa.ch/ |

THAILAND

| | MCT - Music Copyright Thailand | www.mct.in.th/web/mct/index2.php |

THE NETHERLANDS

| | Buma/Stemra | www.bumastemra.nl/en/ |
| | SENA | www.sena.nl/about-sena |

TRINIDAD & TOBAGO

| | COTT - Copyright Music Organisation of Trinidad & Tobago | www.cott.org.tt/ |

TURKEY	
MESAM - Musical Work Owners' Association of Turkey	www.mesam.org.tr/

UKRAINE	
UACRR - Ukrainian Agency of Copyright and Related Rights	uacrr.kiev.ua/?lang=en

URUGUAY	
AGADU - General Association of Authors of Uruguay	

UNITED STATES OF AMERICA	
ASCAP - The American Society of Composers, Authors and Publishers	www.ascap.com/
BMI - Broadcast Music, Inc.	www.bmi.com/about/
SESAC - Society of European Stage Authors & Composers	www.sesac.com/?flash=1
SoundExchange - non-profit performance rights organization	www.soundexchange.com/

Other useful Associations

AGICOA	AGICOA - Global Association of International Collective Management of Audiovisual Works	http://www.agicoa.org/
BIEM	BIEM - Bureau International des Sociétés Gérant les Droits D'Enregistrement et les Reproduction Mecanique	http://www.biem.org/
	CCLI - Christian Copyright Licensing International	http://www.ccli.com/Global.aspx
CISAC	CISAC- International Confederation of Societies of Authors and Composers	http://www.cisac.org/CisacPortal/security.do?method=beforeAuthenticate
ifpi	IFPI - International Federation of the Phonogram Industry	http://www.ifpi.org/
ifrro	IFRRO - International Federation of Reproduction Rights Organisations	http://www.ifrro.org/
SCAPR	SCAPR - The Societies' Council for the Collective Management of Performers' Rights	http://www.scapr.org/

Pitching

"Ever tried. Ever failed. No matter. Try Again. Fail again. Fail better." Samuel Beckett

No matter what kind of Songwriter you are, if you decide you want to place your songs in films, TV, advertisements or would prefer to have another Artist/Band record them, you may come across the term **pitching**.

Pitching is the act of presenting your work to an A&R representative, Publishing House, Music Library or directly to an Artist/Band in the hope that you may persuade them to use your song(s).

If you compose complete songs, meaning that you write the music, lyrics and melody, then you will be able to pitch for work on a solo basis.

However, if you are a Composer of music, it may mean that you will need to work with a Topline Songwriter in order to complete a song that you can pitch as a prospective hit record. If you have Management, they may suggest that you collaborate with a Topline Songwriter who can write a Topline over your musical composition. Many musical partnerships have evolved this way. Any song that a Composer and Topline Songwriter develop together, in collaboration, will be pitched as a collective composition so that both parties receive their agreed share.

In the case of pitching co-written work, you will need to be careful. For instance, let us say you wrote a song with a co-writer but you are no longer in touch with the co-writer. You decide to pitch the track anyway. There are a number of issues which you will have to watch out for:

Firstly, is your co-writer in agreement that your joint work is sent out for pitching? Because the work is a collaborative piece, all respective parties need to concur.

Secondly, you must be clear when pitching what terms you are agreeing to. For example, some work requires 100% of the publishing held on the song. This is fine where the publishing for both collaborators is listed as **copyright control**, but if either co-writer is signed to a Publishing Company, then you will need to clarify whether this song is under contract to a Publishing Company.

Thirdly, it is good business practice to inform your co-writer that you intend to pitch your joint work. Not only does this cover a lot of bases, especially if your co-writer has already submitted the work, or the work may already have been allocated to a company or Artist/Band by your co-writer or their Publishing Company.

What is a Topline?

A **Topline** is a melody written over a piece of music. Usually a Topline Songwriter would write a vocal melody and lyrics, but many Songwriters are both Composer and Topline Songwriter. Some prolific Songwriters specialise in Topline writing and are often used specifically to craft or to complete a song.

Another term for Topline is **Hook**. Both Topline and Hook basically mean the part of a song that you have trouble forgetting and always end up singing along to (usually when you least want to).

Pitching your Topline

As a Songwriter, you may often be asked to write over a track that possibly other Songwriters may also be pitching for.

The problem here is, that if your Topline is rejected, you may be left with a melody that could sound like a lot of other songs.

Equally, it could be seen from a legal standpoint, that the copyright formerly attached to your original Topline may pass over to the completed song once recorded and so effectively, that joint work then becomes copyrighted as a whole itself.

Some Songwriters now send out disclaimers when pitching, stating that if their work is rejected then their Topline and the copyright therein will revert back to them and the musical composition will revert back to the co-writer.

If your work has been rejected, it is a good idea to send a short email to your co-writer, confirming that you will be reusing your Topline on another project. In the same email, acknowledge that your co-writer is equally free to reuse the musical composition for future projects.

One way around the copyright issue would be to use the Topline for another composition but to change parts of the melody and lyrics. Often when you re-use a Topline the new song will have a different chord structure, therefore your song is not wasted and you have worked your way around the copyright issue.

Pitching your Song

Pitching can be hard. The main issue for many Songwriters is having an **out**, somewhere or someone to send their work to. As there are so many Songwriters fighting for the same bite of the cherry, it can take many years for a Songwriter to get even a nibble, but there are lots of avenues that could help you on your way.

A good place to meet people is your local music scene. Open mic nights could be the right setting to approach Artists and Songwriters.

If you have a Publishing Contract, your Publisher may be able to help you with synchronisations and possibly to introduce you to Artists and Songwriters.

Networking is imperative. Attending MIDEM, ADE and other music conferences could have a positive impact, but these events do cost money and unless you have legitimate contacts, you could struggle to arrange meetings. Forward planning running up to the event is necessary to build up your connections, ensuring that you have a few meetings arranged.

There are many websites offering pitching and songwriting services but there is usually a hefty annual fee to join.

In the past, I have used some of these companies but because my published releases did not come through any of these companies, I do not feel I can recommend this route as a real **out** at this point in time. I would suggest that unless you have money to burn, you would be best to try the aforementioned techniques first.

Change a word, get a third

So let us say your song has been accepted by a well-known Artist. You and your co-writers have agreed a 25% split each, but now the Artist is asking for a songwriting credit, even though they did not have anything to do with the writing.

Sometimes Managed Artists (especially those in the higher stratums of the industry) will request a percentage of a song they are going to record, despite having no creative input in the work. This is all very well, except if a song is split four ways and then the Artist decides they want the lion's share, it may feel like you are losing control of your song.

In the case of some major Artists, where a Topline Songwriter has been brought in to write their album, the Artist may have very little creative input, leaving the bulk of the creativity to the Songwriter. However due to the **change a word get a third** tactic, the main Songwriter may feel the rough end of the wedge when they see their ownership and royalty dwindling away, because a star deigns to sing their work but only at a percentage cut.

Most aspiring Songwriters want their songs to be heard, so if it means that Taylor Swift or Robbie Williams want to sing your song, you may just have to forfeit a chunk of your control and royalty percentage, because basically 20% of £1 million could be a nice little earner.

Take Responsibility

O for a Muse of fire, that would ascend, the brightest heaven of invention, a Kingdom for a stage, princes to act and Monarchs to behold the swelling scene! (William Shakespeare: Henry V)

I t has taken me a long time to realise that there is no easy option. When I have tried a quick fix or relied on someone do a task that I could have effectively carried out myself, they have done very little and charged me an enormous fee for the privilege or done very little and damaged my career.

So my advice is to take full responsibility for your own career. Learn your trade well, at least to the best of your knowledge and capability. Study how the industry works.

Develop yourself

This may sound a strange thing to say, but you need to **develop yourself**. After all, you are the package, you are the brand, and if you do not have the back-up of a Record Label to do this for you, this is something you will have to do yourself.

These days, it seems as if there are a lot more Bands and Artists for the consumer to pick and choose from. Competition is high, which effectively means you must be individual, play up your strengths, whilst presenting them in a realistic yet convincing manner.

Logos/Branding/ORM

Logos and branding are another way to get noticed. Due to the rapid growth of the internet and social media sites, you will need to be ahead of the game when it comes to managing your image/brand/logo online. There are companies that offer Online Reputation Management (**ORM**), but this is likely to be fee based and if you are just starting out you may not want to spend money in this area. However, you can still design your own logo/branding. Another way to interact with your fans would be to hold competitions for logo design and/or artwork for your tracks.

Selling your merchandise

Great marketing is the key to selling your merchandise. For instance, offer your fans a one-off vinyl edition EP or a special edition digital album, downloadable with alternative mixes.

Remember, everyone loves a bargain so try offering your fans **two for one** deals on tracks.

You need to connect with your fans which will, in turn, help them to stay connected to you. Let fans know who you are and engage them by getting them involved in any way you can. Fans appreciate having their loyalty repaid especially if you are offering them exclusive deals.

CDs, Vinyl or tracks that can only be purchased via your website with serial numbers (i.e. 1 of 100 copies), creates an image that you are offering a special edition or collector's piece just for your die-hard fans.

Another option would be to offer your fans free music, free tickets to your gigs or band paraphernalia in exchange for them promoting you. Or you can offer different versions of your new single; an early recording, a specialist DJ remix or an acoustic / live recording for any fans that help to get your Facebook or Twitter count up.

Mailing List

Start a mailing list, learn how to add people and how best to use it to promote your work, merchandise and events.

Try something different

Do something exciting and different. **Trent Reznor** of **Nine Inch Nails** is a great advocate of using different formats to market his work. He had a great idea which went viral when he planted unmarked memory sticks in bathrooms at his concerts for fans to find.

Interact / Competitions / Offers

Offer fans a chance to a remix one of your tracks. A lot of Record Labels do this as a cheap way of getting a fresh and exciting remix from an up and coming new Producer.

Going Live

Everyone seems to be making films these days and as most mobile phones have some form of video application, it is not hard to make a short film and upload instantly to websites or YouTube. This is such a simple but effect way to engage with your fans.

Film yourself recording a track or for the next interview you have been asked to do, do it live. Take footage of shows or things you think your fans would be interested in. Again, if you do not have money for a professional video this is another avenue for a competition for fans to interact with you.

The Back-Up Plan

Forewarned, forearmed; to be prepared is half the victory. (Miguel de Cervantes - Don Quixote)

Not wishing to dampen your creative spirits but without a hit record or a trust fund, you will need to make provision for your future. With the ever-changing dynamic of the Music Industry, even some of the most established Artists/Bands have found they have been unable to rest upon their laurels. After years of living the high life, some are now looking at a life of penury.

As an Artist, you will be self-employed. This means not only do you have to be responsible for your own accounts, but you will have no company pension, healthcare scheme or a guaranteed monthly salary. Without a regular monthly income, either through royalties or paid work, you may find yourself somewhat destitute.

So when you do get an advance or a royalty cheque, it is worth getting a few areas of your financial life into gear.

Personal Pension

As a Singer/Songwriter, you are likely to be self-employed. This means that you will have to personally make provision for your retirement. Investing in a formal pension arrangement is both structured and tax efficient. However, pension legislation is not easy to understand and changes regularly, so professional advice is essential. The earlier you start saving into a pension plan, the bigger your income will be on your retirement.

Savings/Investments

As with a Personal Pension, the earlier you start to save the better, that is, provided you are able to leave your savings to mature over some years. If you are lucky enough to get a big royalty pay out, then this would be the time to invest your money, rather than spending most of it, in the vain hope that there is more to come. Life is often full of curve balls and surprises. Financial success does not always go hand in hand with fame.

You will therefore need to **make hay while the sun shines**.

In the words of **Warren Buffet**:

> *Do not save what is left after spending,*
> *spend what is left after saving.*

Career

For some, it is often the case that a second job has to be attained in order to fund the dream role of Singer/Songwriter.

Many Artists/Bands have put themselves through school and University, attaining qualifications for a secondary (primarily, a career path that acts as their fall-back) profession.

Although, in the case of **Queen's Brian May**, he became a rockstar in 1970 first and then attained his Ph.D. in astrophysics from Imperial College in 2007.

Tax

As an Artist, you will be self-employed and therefore will have to fill in your own tax returns or pay an accountant to do this for you. Do not rely on your Record Label to pay the tax due on your royalty statements or advances. If your Record Label, Publisher or Management send you a payment and they confirm they have not withheld tax on your behalf, your next step would be to get advice from an accountant or your local Tax Office.

Financial Advice

Being self-employed may mean that you do not have a **benefits package** that many employers now provide for their staff. In addition to a Pension, a typical package might include cover for: Life Assurance, Personal Injury, Private Medical Healthcare, Dental Care and Critical Illness, amongst other things.

Some of these benefits may not be affordable, nor applicable, but a Financial Adviser will be able to explain their potential value to you. When consulting any Adviser, always use someone who comes recommended either by a trusted source or a personal contact.

Parthian Shot

"With which Parthian shot he walked away, leaving the two rivals open-mouthed behind him."—Sir Arthur Conan Doyle

At the wonderful age of 24, I had the opportunity of meeting with two well-known Producers of the time, whom I held in high regard. These Producers had been blessed with a string of hits throughout the 80s. Unlike the many casualties of the one hit wonder brigade, swallowed up and fading into the oblivion of the next era, these two had the luxury of resting most adeptly on their laurels. I was so delighted that they had very kindly taken the time to impart some of their infinite wisdom upon me.

I was nervous but excited to meet them both. They were older, wiser and I reckoned probably, twice my age. They looked me up and down and without hearing a single note, informed me that at the grand old age of 24, I was already **too old** for the music industry.

You can imagine I felt deflated and like the bottom had fallen out of my world.

In fact when I look back at the interview now, (if you can call it an interview for it was so short), I wish I had given them a proverbial **Parthian shot.** Alas, at 24 years young, I was extremely shy and believed that people such as these knew better than me.

Thankfully, their advice did not deter me.

So one thing I want to impress upon you here is this. **NOBODY**, utterly and absolutely, **NO-ONE** has the right to be rude to you, to be dismissive, to make you feel degraded in any way.

To be an Artist, a Musician, a Creative, you **do not** have to look a certain way, be a certain size, be a certain shape, be a certain colour. You do not have to do **certain** things. You just have to be **you**.

I feel that the Music Industry today has dived even further into the depths of amoral and misogynistic values, exploiting many, making them feel devalued.

Some may argue that these men and women are in control, but I disagree and I feel that as time passes by, their biographies will reveal a darkness, encapsulated within tales of troubled souls. This kind of manipulation is extremely damaging. Any psychologist will tell you, that if you are reminded time and time again that you should look a certain way or that you are not good enough, eventually you may start to believe it and that is not right. The most important rule is **be true to you**.

Many of the great artists, such as, Van Gogh and Mozart, experienced their own artistic madness and died penniless for the privilege. But they produced some of the most inimitably inspiring work despite being against the odds.

If faced with the dilemma of **selling ones soul** to be famous and a possibility of making bundles of money, you will need to ask yourself whether your artistry and your integrity have a price.

It seems most these days would say everyone has a price …

... or is that just the devil talking?

Protection and Pitfalls

"Innocence always calls mutely for protection when we would be so much wiser to guard ourselves against it: innocence is like a dumb leper who has lost his bell, wandering the world, meaning no harm." —Graham Greene

Pitfall

You have been asked to sing another Songwriter's songs, you feel this may limit your opportunities of becoming a Songwriter and you are not being offered any publishing royalty.

Protection

It should ultimately be your decision should you decide to sing another Songwriter's work. However, it is best to have a few paragraphs set out ready for prospective offers, stating that you normally only collaborate as a Songwriter. You can then adapt this paragraph should you choose to sing for a Songwriter. It would also be prudent, when sending this wording, to take the opportunity to agree the splits and publishing percentage, if any is on offer. If you are not clear in your negotiations, but instead presume you will get a positive outcome, then you may be greatly disappointed. It is always best to be open and to ask for the deal to be set out in writing.

🎭 Pitfall

You are continually being listed as **featuring** on tracks, despite the fact that you have co-written the songs. You feel mislead and disrespected.

🎭 Protection

From the offset of a collaboration, all your correspondence and any collaboration agreement should set out the track listing, stating that you are not a **featured** artist but that you are an equal party, i.e. Artist **and** Artist. Should the third party continue to use the term **featuring**, you can bring this to their attention and advise them that they are legally bound to use the title you agreed upon in the initial stages of the collaboration.

🎭 Pitfall

You decided to join a Band and the guitarist is insisting on writing all the songs. Despite them being great songs, you are unsure as your position when it comes to royalties and publishing.

🎭 Protection

As you are not writing the songs, the guitarist does not have **ANY** obligation to pay you for your contribution to the songs, unless you have kept proof of your input or had the foresight to sign a songwriting/collaboration agreement, setting out your percentage share of the songwriting. So before things go any further, sit down and work out your splits.

🎭 Pitfall

You have worked as a Singer / Session Singer and in a recent session created a hook or adlibs that completely shaped or reinvented the song. The Songwriter is passing you off and has refused to offer you a percentage of the track.

🎭 Protection

If you feel that you are being badly treated, it is good to remember that the intellectual property vested in your vocal belongs to you. If the Songwriter refuses to acknowledge your creative input, you always have the option of refusing to let your vocal or melody be used and see where your negotiations go from there.

🎭 Pitfall

Good news! You have been asked to attend an audition, however, before you can attend, they have asked you for a fee to cover their costs.

🎭 Protection

No *bona fide* company will ask you to pay to attend an audition or session.

Pitfall

You have been asked to attend an audition and are unsure as to the correct protocol.

Protection

NEVER visit **ALONE**, always take someone with you, tell someone where you are going and/or leave the address you are attending with someone. You should never feel pressured to have to attend or to be alone with someone you do not know. It may be someone you do know but you are uncomfortable being on your own with them. Remember: your safety and security is paramount.

Pitfall

You have a new Manager and he is sending to you Timbuktu to perform at a gig alone.

Protection

I cannot stress the importance of safety. If you decide to tour, it is imperative to have a chaperone (especially if you are a single woman). The travelling and waiting can be lonely and tiring, so insist on bringing a companion under the guise of an **Assistant**.

Pitfall

You have been networking and a Producer is insistent that he can make you a **star**. However, there are certain provisos attached to his promise which you feel are not really in keeping within the bounds of a professional relationship.

Protection

Keep your career professional at all times. **NEVER** believe in flannel i.e. **I can make you a star** because usually it comes to naught and there is always a price to pay. No service as such is ever free and you will usually find that the word that follows **I can make you a star** is usually **if....** *If you pretend to be my partner, if you just do this* and so on.

Pitfall

You have just co-written a song with a Songwriter through the internet. The Songwriter keeps writing tweets on Twitter and posting on Facebook giving out links to this new track. You are unhappy because the track is not finalised and no deal has been agreed.

Protection

You should have agreed your splits prior to the collaboration, so you should own a percentage of it. You are entitled to tell your co-writer that you are not happy about the song being shared with the public until it has been signed. Also a prospective Record Label may not want the track to have been heard before they are ready to promote it.

Pitfall

You have collaborated and sung a song which has been signed by a Record Label. The co-writer is using an old photo of you on various social media sites. It is not a picture you would like used and are unhappy about it.

Protection

Although there is no general right protecting image under UK law, copyright may be viewed as being breached by the use of an unauthorised photograph. The first call of action would be to contact the co-writer and give them a photo you are happy using and also put in writing that you wish them to take the original photo down from all the sites it has been posted on.

If they do not take the original photo down or refuse to abide by your wishes, then your secondary action would be to try to get the photo removed, which on sites like Facebook can be a simple procedure. In stating that you own the intellectual property of the image and have not given the co-writer permission to use it, may be enough to have the respective sites remove it on your behalf.

Lastly, if the co-writer is still refusing to adhere to your wishes, an email or letter to the co-writer, setting out that you intend to seek professional advice with regard to the removal of the image, may be enough to propel the co-writer into corrective action. However, if this approach still fails, you may have to seek advice from a professional.

Pitfall

You have just signed a Management Contract because you feel overwhelmed with paper and you have several collaboration contracts that you do not understand and cannot be bothered to look at.

Protection

Never assume that a Manager has a Degree in entertainment law or that Management employs a Solicitor who specialises in entertainment law. Before signing a Management Contract clarify who will explain and deal with any contracts for you.

Pitfall

You have just had your first track released and people are taking notice of you, including Management. You have been asked to sign a Management Contract what should you do?

Protection

Before signing, as with **ALL** contracts, get a Solicitor to look over it. Some Management Contracts are over complicated and may contain legally binding restrictions, whereby even if your Management no longer represents you, they are still entitled to a percentage of your earnings. This may be on a reducing percentage scale and can be up to a ten year period after termination, so it is imperative to read the small print carefully.

Pitfall

You have discussed a new idea for a book with your Manager and he seemed very interested. So much that he has just asked you to sign another contract.

Protection

Management may ask you to sign a provision which binds you into a Contract, allowing a percentage of any other fiscal gain made from any creative sources. Unless your Management has credible contacts of benefit to you and most importantly you are happy to pay a percentage for this new service, then there is no good reason to sign another Contract or assign any extra rights over to Management. If you do decide to sign a new Contract, get it checked over and watch out for these pitfalls. Do not feel pressured into signing a new Contract without first getting advice.

Pitfall

You have been researching and so far everyone you meet has an idea of the best route to success. Most want to charge for their knowledge or refer you to a website and/or third party, but again this is at a cost.

Protection

There are a lot of people ready and willing to take your hard earned cash. Always research any ideas or introductions. There is a wealth of information on the internet in chat rooms and forums that will help you to distinguish the good from the bad.

Pitfall

You have been offered an Artist Development Deal but from looking at the Contract it does not look like a great deal is on the table. What should you do?

Protection

With the wealth of talent at the fingertips of most Major Record Labels, an Artist Development deal is often the first Contract offered to a new Artist. Nonetheless, these contracts can be fuelled with high royalties in favour of the Record Label and often contain provisions whereby an Artist/Band loses their rights because the Record Label intends to develop their profile.

First of all, get advice from a Solicitor. The chances are, the deal may not be all you had hoped for, but it may start you on your way. You will need to weigh up all the pros and cons and decide whether it is worth forfeiting some of your rights and royalties. It may be that you would prefer to go it alone or wait for a better offer.

Often the first Contract is a **tempter** and once negotiations are underway, a better deal may be offered. As always, if you do not ask you are unlikely to get. You will need to negotiate, especially if you wish to keep certain rights.

Useful Addresses

"Would you tell me, please, which way I ought to go from here? That depends a good deal on where you want to get to, said the Cat. I don't much care where, said Alice. Then it doesn't matter which way you go, said the Cat. So long as I get somewhere, Alice added as an explanation." (Lewis Carroll - Alice's Adventures in Wonderland)

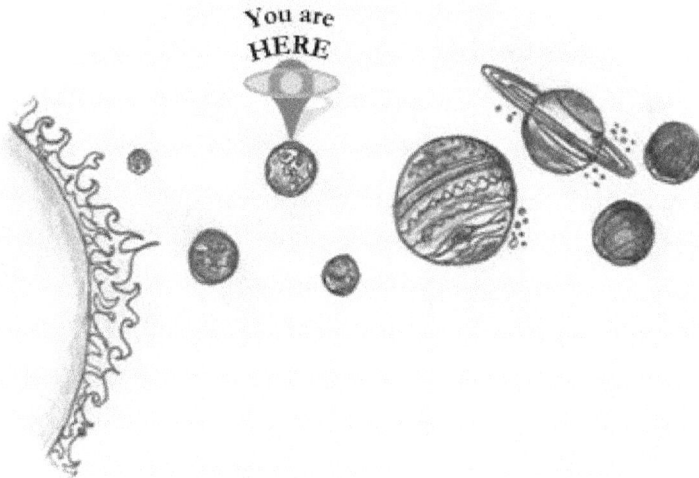

ADE (Amsterdam Dance Event)
http://www.amsterdam-dance-event.nl/

Apple
http://www.apple.com/uk/

BASCA
2nd Floor, British Music House
26 Berners Street
London
W1T 3LR
Tel: 020 7636 2929
Email: info@basca.org.uk
http://basca.org.uk/

Copyright Licensing Agency
Saffron House
6-10 Kirby Street
London
EC1N 8TS
Tel: 020 7400 3100
www.cla.co.uk

Cubase
Steinberg Media Technologies GmbH
Frankenstr. 18 b
20097 Hamburg
Germany
Tel: 00 49 (0)40 210 35-0
Fax: 00 49 (0)40 210 35-300
http://www.steinberg.net/en/home.html

Equity
Head Office London
Guild House
Upper St Martins Lane
London
WC2H 9EG
Tel: 020 7379 6000
Email: info@equity.org.uk
http://www.equity.org.uk/home/

FAC (Featured Artists Coalition)
Unit 41, Tileyard Studios
Tileyard Road
London
N7 9AH
Tel: 020 7700 5755
Email: info@thefac.org
http://thefac.org/

Intellectual Property Office
Concept House
Cardiff Road
Newport
South Wales
NP10 8QQ
Tel: 0300 300 2000
www.ipo.gov.uk

ISM (Incorporated Society of Musicians)
4–5 Inverness Mews
London
W2 3JQ
Tel: 020 7221 3499
Email: membership@ism.org
http://www.ism.org/

MIDEM (Marché International du Disque et de l'Edition Musicale)
http://www.midem.com/

MU (Musicians' Union)
60-62 Clapham Road
London
SW9 0JJ
Tel: 020 7582 5566
Email: info@theMU.org
http://www.musiciansunion.org.uk/

MUSIC WEEK
Suncourt House
18-26 Essex Road
Islington
London
N1 8LN
Tel: 020 7226 7246
http://www.musicweek.com/

NME (New Musical Express)
9th Floor
Blue Fin Building
London
SE1 0SU
http://www.nme.com/

PRS for Music
29-33 Berners Street
London
W1P 4AA
Tel. 020 7580 5544
www.prsformusic.com

PPLUK
1 Upper James Street
London
W1F 9DE
Tel 020 7534 1000
www.ppluk.com
info@ppluk.com

Sylvia Young Agency
Sylvia Young Theatre School
1 Nutford Place
London
W1H 5YZ
Tel: 020 7723 0037
www.sylviayoungtheatreschool.co.uk
info@sylviayoungtheatreschool.co.uk

The BRIT School for the Performing Arts & Technology
60 The Crescent
Croydon
CR0 2HN
Tel: 020 8665 5242
www.brit.croydon.sch.uk
admin@brit.croydon.sch.uk

The Italia Conti Academy of Theatre Arts Limited
Italia Conti House
23 Goswell Road
London EC1M 7AJ
Tel: 020 7608 0044
www.italiaconti.com
admin@italiaconti.co.uk.com

For enquiries about Acting Courses please contact:
The Italia Conti Academy of Theatre Arts Limited
Avondale
72 Landor Road
London SW9 9PH
Tel: 020 7733 3210
acting@italiaconti.co.uk

The Stage
Stage House
47 Bermondsey Street
London SE1 3XT
Tel: 0207403 1818
www.thestage.co.uk

The X Factor
https://application.xfactor.tv/

Index

www.ingramcontent.com/pod-product-compliance
Lightning Source LLC
Chambersburg PA
CBHW080855090426
42733CB00013B/2494